THE HR COMPANION

Human Resource Management

DR. LAMIN TOMBEKAI KAMARA

ARPress

ARPress
45 Dan Road Suite 5
Canton MA 02021
Hotline: 1(888) 821-0229
Fax: 1(508) 545-7580

Ordering Information:
Quantity sales. Special discounts are available on quantity purchases by corporations, associations, and others. For details, contact the publisher at the address above.

Printed in the United States of America.

ISBN-13:   Softcover   979-8-89389-787-6
                  eBook   979-8-89389-788-3

Library of Congress Control Number: 2024923414

TABLE OF CONTENTS

Acknowledgment

I'd like to acknowledge the below listed individuals for their vast contributions to the publishing of this book. They in many ways dedicated their talents and hard work for me to succeed throughout my research and up to the publication. I will always remember them for their invaluable advice and sleepless nights they set aside at any time I call upon them. I will forever remember you all. Thanks a-lot.

Dr. Nick E. Bradford

Dr. Keith Dodson

Neile Nardi Ashard

Benjamin Clinton

Prof. Ben McCarty

Dr. Diego Gonzalez

Dr. Nancy Cabperson

Mike Myerson

Francis Miskin-Mass

Fernando Castillano

Birdford Hernandez

Dr. Miskin Mass

Nailando Nelson

Juvenile Declaw

Nick and Marie Miskin

Hanson P. Matthews

Dr. Balak Ibn-Qualim

The Human Resource Companion Is your ticket to a better control of your Human Resource Office of one practitioner. Perfect for every aspect of the control you visualize, making perfect decisions and providing for those you work.

PUBLISHER
Dr. Lamin Tombekai Kamara

PROOFREADER
Dr. Nick E. Bradford

TECHNICAL READER
Dr. Diph Dodson

CONTRIBUTORS
Neile Nardi Ashard
Benjamin Clinton
Prof. Ben McCarty
Diego Guevera
Nancy Cabperson
Mike Myerson
Francis Miskin-Mass
Fernando Castillo
Bradford Hernandez
Miskin Mass

PEER REVIEWERS
Nailando Nelson
Juvenile Declaw

COPY READER
Nick and Marie Nalando

COMPOSITION LAYOUT
Hanson P. Matthews
Dr. Balak Ibn-Qualim

DEDICATION

This book is dedicated to:

KD, the children and

My late Uncle, Alhaji Maddie Conteh; my mother, my late father, my sisters and Magdaline Jebbeh Johnson

PREFACE

My definition of Human Resource is "The people that staff and operate an organization…as contrasted with the financial and material resources of an organization. The organizational function that deals with the people…" Long a term used sarcastically by individuals in the line organization, because it relegates humans to the same category as financial and material resources, human resources will be replaced by more customer-friendly terms in the future.

The reason for choosing this topic emanates from the vast experience I achieved in recent times while working in Human Resource Organizations in a short time but numerous Human Resource offices also. This book should help to make you a perfect HR practitioner in an office run by one person. Publishing this book will help many HR Practitioners like you to turn their time in managing people and soliciting perfect employment for the organizations they work. This book is an encyclopedic directory, synthesized and carefully written in every aspect of Human Resource Development circles, from employment to budget management, enabling the reader to grasp the profits of these scribes concerning the benevolence of perfect HR office operations.

The most effective information about Human Resource within this book are the bulleted statements, which should be carefully considered as very important factors. They provide the best information an HR practitioner might need to run his/her office. Other pertinent information are supportive to the bulleted statements and they also contribute perfect meanings for understanding the literature hereunto that states.

The Indexes this book contains are very rich; they also reveal the most important forms an HR practitioner might need to successfully run his/her office.

Personnel management is a responsibility of all who manage people as well as being a description of the work of those who are employed as specialists. It is that part of management which is concerned with people at work and with their relationships within an enterprise. Personnel management aims to achieve both efficiency and justice, neither of which can be pursued successfully without the other. It seeks to bring together and develop into an effective organization the men and women who make up an enterprise, enabling each to make his own best contribution to its success both as an individual and as a member of a working group. It seeks to provide fair terms and conditions of employment and satisfying work for those employed.

CHAPTER ONE

WHO IS THE HR AND WHAT ARE HIS FUNCTIONS?

Congratulations. You have just chosen one of the best literatures in Human Resource Management studies; a new and very summarized reading for the excellent advantage of how to deal and treat the employee and management team of your organization. You have been assigned one of the most critical functions in your company. You are now responsible for the people-oriented policies and procedures in your organization. In many ways, the future success of your company lies with you.

Your job is anything but simple. At first glance, the magnitude of all your new challenges may seem overwhelming. However, every challenge presents a corresponding opportunity for you to take and maintain a strong leadership position in your company.

You were chosen for this position for a reason. You have demonstrated that you are able to cope with multiple priorities. You have also exhibited how you can be trusted. Your company's management team wanted a Human Resources professional who could serve the needs of employees, management, and shareholders. Since valuable management of these three areas is critical to the future success of your company, you are well positioned to become a strong leadership role model if you accept the challenges and pursue the opportunities vigorously.

Your Know-how set

Let's take a look at some of the skills and characteristics that are necessary to successfully fulfill the Human Resource professional's role. By choosing you for this position, your management team has expressed confidence that you possess these skills:

- **Organization**. HR requires an organized and orderly approach. Organized files, good time management, and personal efficiency are essential to the HR function. For example, managers want timely access to accurate personnel files, and they need advice on compensation and workplace features such as flextime.

- **Multitasking**. Unaccompanied professionals are likely to be handling an employee's personal issue 1 minute, a benefit claim the next, and a recruiting strategy for a hard-to-fill engineering job the minute after that. Priorities and business needs change fast, and you'll need to change with them.

- **Discretion and Ethics.** HR is the conscience of the company, as well as the repository of confidential information. Along with speaking the language and serving the needs of top management, you will monitor management's approach to employees to ensure that proper business ethics are observed. The HR professional must push back whenever it's necessary to keep the whole firm on the straight and narrow. And you will be responsible for handling appropriately—never divulging to the wrong parties—confidential information about everyone in the organization.

- **A dual focus.** HR professionals need to consider the needs of both employees and management. Employees need to trust HR. They look for confidentiality and expect HR to advocate for their concerns. Yet HR must also advocate for enforcing top management's policies. This can be a difficult balancing act.

- **Fairness.** Successful HR professionals demonstrate fairness and inspire trust. However, fairness doesn't mean that everyone must be treated equally. Rather, it means that communication is clear, that peoples' voices are heard, that laws are followed, and that privacy and respect is maintained.

- **A focus on training and continuous improvement.** HR professionals need to help managers coach and develop their employees. The goal is continued improvement and innovation as well as remediation.

- **A Strategic orientation.** Forward-thinking HR professionals take a leadership role and influence the strategic path that management takes. It's part of HR's responsibility to ensure that the organization flourishes and avoids problems.

- **A team orientation.** HR must understand the dynamics of teams and find ways to make them work. That's because most companies today are often organized into teams, rather than into hierarchies headed by supervisors and managers.

Your Functions and Tasks

What are the specific roles and responsibilities of the HR professional in a department of one? The answer to that question has changed dramatically in the past few years. In the current climate, businesses have flatter organizations, more diversity, greater numbers of temporary and contract workers, a team-based structure, a better-educated workforce, and a customer-driven service economy. In addition, workers tend to be more mobile and less loyal, with several generations represented in the workplace at once. It is not unusual for a worker to change jobs every 2 years or so, especially in countries where industrialization is so rudimentary, war stricken and desolate.

So, given these factors, the HR function covers a wide variety of responsibilities. There are administrative duties, such as keeping accurate records of what the organization is doing and what its employees are doing. There are training and development activities, such as workshops and the continuing education of workers. There are issues with benefits, such as researching and implementing employee insurance and other benefits. And there are legal issues, such as ensuring that the organization is complying with all employment, safety, and health laws, an issue which third-world countries need to address.

- Essentially, HR management plays a pivotal role in:

- Developing strategies to make sure the organization has the people it needs to meet short—and long—term goals.

- Creating and communicating organizational policies and practices
- Ensuring the organization complies with employment and safety laws
- Keeping thorough records and ensuring confidentiality
- Attracting, retaining, developing, and motivating excellent employees
- Communicating with and training employees and managers
- Developing and implementing a fair and equitable compensation system
- Improving job performance, increasing quality and quantity of work
- Developing and implementing a fair and legal disciplinary system
- Discharging poor performers
- Auditing HR departmental effectiveness
- Contributing to the organization's strategic planning

The HR's Everyday's Functions

As a one-person HR practitioner in an organization, you can expect to spend about 40 percent of your day handling questions, attending budgeting and strategic planning meetings, and interviewing prospective employees. The rest of your time will most likely be spent on administrative matters such as contacting service providers (payroll, healthcare insurance, bank officers, etc.) and managing paper flow and records.

You will be called on to take the lead when there is a workplace conflict or deal with a difficult or unsympathetic boss or supervisor who is creating headaches for you. You might come into work expecting a calm day and encounter a workplace emergency.

The most difficult feature of the HR professional's job is handling the difficult interpersonal challenges involved in the staffing of a company. Some people call it "dirty work" of HR—dealing with understaffing, refereeing disputes between mismatched personalities, firing employees, informing employees of small (or nonexistent) bonuses, and reprimanding irresponsible employees for drunkenness, bad character, abusiveness and some other odds.

Performing these tasks can be disheartening for HR managers, who want to support and assist employees rather than discipline them. In other cases, HR managers are termed to be babysitters and many more HR managers regret that employees dislike, fear, or avoid them because of this role. It can be a lonely road. "What do you do when your job is to keep in touch with the company's needs, but no one wants to meet with you?" wrote one HR professional.

Remind yourself once again that you are in HR because you are skilled at jumping over hurdles and solving interpersonal problems, including family and other relationships. Your role isn't to make everyone like you. You won't win all your battles, and there will be some people who don't like you, despite your best efforts to be fair and honest.

Your main missions are to gauge and fill the labor needs of your company; help to attract and retain the most qualified employees; fulfill employee financial, benefits-related, and psychological needs; and weather the economy through good management of benefits. That's a fairly comprehensive list of duties. Are you up for the challenge?

You're going to need to bestride the fence between the "soft" and "hard" sides of the business. It's the nature of your job. But if you have to ultimately pick a side, here are the watchwords: *Think and act strategically at all times if you want to be a player!*

Take things one step at a time. Remember that you are not alone in this— even if you are a one person practitioner. This book will walk you through the basics and refer you to other resources that you can tap into. So take a deep breath and hold on. You are in for an interesting ride!

How Should the Unaccompanied HR Practitioner Begin?

The unaccompanied HR practitioner is unique in that he or she is probably charged with the overall HR responsibilities for a firm with between 50 and 150 employees. This means that the RH professional in a smaller firm becomes a jack-of-all-trades. He or she is involved in hiring, resource allocation, compensation, benefits, compliance with laws affecting employees and the workplace, and safety and health issues.

This multiplicity of tasks requires individuals with strong organizational skills who can quickly shift from project to project and topic to topic without becoming overwhelmed.

A good first step for the new unaccompanied HR practitioner would be to quickly learn HR jargon and develop a network of people and resources that you can turn to when you have questions or problems. You probably won't have the luxury of any down time, so be prompt and aggressive about gaining needed skills and knowledge.

Access the Resources You Need

Here are some ways to get up to speed and start building your HR resources network:

- **Buy books and subscribe to resources.** The fact that you bought this book demonstrates that you are already on track for your self- education initiative. There are many other excellent books, manuals, newsletters, journals, and electronic resources available to HR professionals. Some offer depth in a particular area such as employee relations or compliance issues.

- **Join the local and national chapters of trade associations.** For example, one highly recommended group is the Society for Human Resource Management (SHRM). It is the world's largest association devoted to human resources management. Representing more than 200,000 individual members, SHRM's mission is both to serve human resources management professionals and to advance the profession.

- **Prepare to obtain HR certification.** A quick online search will point you to numerous resources to learn about certification. Certification can be achieved at many colleges or can even be obtained online. Some programs are better than others, so it would be wise to check with SHRM, WorldatWork, or other professional groups to ascertain that you are getting the best training available.

- **Use the Internet.** If you have a question about the Family and Medical Leave Act (FMLA) in the United States of America or the Americans with Disabilities Act (ADA)— or virtually any legislation or compliance issue—general information is readily available online. Your initial goal is to become conversant, but as you face new challenges, you can get online any time to tap into information or answer a question that comes up for you. You may also want to sign up for free e-mail newsletters, such as BLR's HR Daily Advisor, that are available at such sites as HR Daily Advisor.blr.com. These will alert you to new developments in the HR field and to important deadlines that you need to observe for filing paperwork, etc.

- **Call colleagues for advice.** Developing a network is probably one of the most worthwhile activities you can pursue during your first days as HR manager. Don't hesitate to call an HR professional in a company of similar size—even if you don't know the person—for guidance and advice. You'll find that HR professionals are a very friendly, open, and helpful group. Few questions are off-limits. You can also be sure that HR people know how to maintain confidentiality, so you can rest assured that they will honor your privacy just as you will honor theirs.

- **Visit the libraries of area business schools.** Need some help with team building or leadership? Are you looking to learn business terminology or budgeting so that you can be a strategic member of the management team? You'll find a wealth of material at area community colleges and business schools that you won't find online or in public libraries. You may even be able to arrange an appointment with a professor or graduate student who can advise you on a specific question.

Although you may be the lone HR person at your company, you don't need to go it alone. Advice is just a phone call or mouse click away!

Seasoned in Human Resources—New in Small HR Department

Perhaps you are not new to the Human Resources profession, and some of what I have talked about is already familiar to you. But even if you are not new to the profession, being a lone HR practitioner is certainly a new experience!

If you came from a larger organization, chances are you specialized in one area, such as compensation, hiring, or resource allocation. If you were a compensation analyst, you worked with department managers to determine pay scales and bonus structures, among other activities. If you were a hiring specialist (also known as a recruiter), you placed ads in appropriate publications and on online job-sites, reviewed resume, and interviewed candidates for employment. If you were an allocation manager, you matched assistants, support staff, and other employees with departments that had specific needs.

In your former capacity, you probably never had to tackle the full spectrum of HR responsibilities. An "HR department of one" does it all. That doesn't mean that he or she has to actually execute every task—there is always outsourcing—but the generalist must have an eye on the big picture at all times.

Certainly, your background will be an asset. You know the lingo, and you know the pitfalls. You'll be aware of such necessities as posting notices required by the federal Occupational Safety and Health Administration (OSHA) and the U.S. Department of Labor (DOL). However, at some point you will probably "hit the wall" with other responsibilities and you may feel as though you are in over your head.

Take a look at this as a seasoned professional

- Draw upon everything you learned as part of a larger HR department, but be open to the time-, energy-, and cost-saving techniques this book has to offer.

- Don't spend too much time in your comfort zone. It's natural to want to do those safe tasks the ones you are most familiar with from your former job. You're the show now, so make sure you step outside your personal comfort zone and give equal—or more—time to less familiar aspects of the job.

- Keep in touch with your professional network. Your former colleagues and the contacts you've made from your "prior life" will be a great help as you get your bearings in your new job.

The Human Resources Today

There has seldom been a more exciting time to be in HR! While HR shares, with other business units, the challenge of doing more with less, it is becoming more widely recognized as a key part of the corporate strategic team. That's the result of HR's increasing focus on streamlining day-t0-day activities so that you have the time for strategic initiatives. This section looks at HR's emerging role as a strategic business partner and how you, as a one practitioner, can match your objectives to your company's mission.

The Changing Face of the Workplace

The international workforce has always evolved, but today, those changes seem to be happening at a breakneck pace with no function unaffected. HR is finding itself at the center of this, trying to cope with changes that have already occurred while preparing for changes that are coming. As you survey your organization, you'll most likely see 10 trends that affect your job:

1. Flatter organizations. Fewer middle managers mean that responsibility and accountability have been pushed down to employees. When filling staffing vacancies, you need to hire talented people who are self-directed and have good organizational as well as technical skills.

2. Growing diversity. The entry of more women, minorities, and immigrants into the workforce has not just changed the face of the workplace; it has also affected what types of benefits and training you offer in order to remain an employer of choice.

3. More temporary and contract workers. With tight controls on headcount, employers are increasingly turning to temps for maximum flexibility. Integrating these mobile workers into your organization can present a unique set of challenges.

4. Greater mobility. You may find that more of your employees are willing to take short-term assignments out of town or relocate to other facilities. Employees are also more willing to switch jobs within a company in order to build their resumes.

5. Less loyalty. Lifetime employment is no longer a given. The waves of layoffs, downsizings, and facility closings have contributed to the trend of employees staying at a job for a short period, then moving on. This is a double-edged sword: You may be challenged to hang onto your best employees, but you also may have a broader talent pool to draw on when you do have an opening.

6. Team-based organizations. Many companies are organized into teams rather than hierarchies headed by supervisors and managers. When recruiting, you need to hire people who have a team orientation.

7. A customer-driven economy. The shift of jobs from the manufacturing sector to the service sector means that organizations must respond to customers as never before. Every employee needs to understand and internalize this customer-driven focus.

8. A better-educated workforce. Better-educated employees are often more assertive. Expect employees to want to have a say in how the organization is run.

9. Smaller companies. The trend toward smaller companies has also accelerated the trend to one person HR practitioners.

10. Information-driven environments. Information can now be obtained, shared, and disseminated almost instantaneously. New employees need to understand how to use this access to information to help them in their jobs. You may find that job descriptions are impacted by this trend, and you can't afford to ignore its implications, especially when recruiting, hiring, and training.

Aligning the HR Agenda with Your Company's Needs

How can you ensure that what the company needs is what you provide? Here's how HR practitioners throughout the world are responding to their companies' mandates to do more with less: less money, fewer people, and fewer hassles.

- Partnering with senior managers to improve employee performance. This may mean developing new systems to reward top performers and weeding out those who cannot meet performance improvement goals.

- Identifying new technology that will streamline functions cost- effectively. Upgrading human resources information systems (HRIS), while expensive, will pay off in the long run.

- Outstanding functions where it makes tactical sense

- Eliminating functions, practices, and procedures that have become obsolete no matter how entrenched they are.

- Working with line managers to identify the skills and competencies needed in today's workers and tomorrow's new hires, and implementing training and recruiting that will fill those needs.

- The willingness to cut budgets, share the pain of other departments, and look for innovative solutions is one way to prove that your goals are aligned with your organization's goals.

Two Keys to Building Credibility and Influence

HR professionals who play a significant role on the senior management team say their success is a combination of vision, ability, and a strong understanding of the company's culture, technology, and business structure. Here are two key strategies that have worked for them—and can work for you:

1. Ask challenging questions. It's not enough to ask, "You want what by when?" You also have to ask "Why?" For example: "Why can't we outsource this project rather than try to hire 10 qualified temps by next week for a 3-week assignment?" Equally as important as asking strategic questions, however, is listening carefully to the answers. Each time you ask "WHY," you have the opportunity to learn more about the way your business really works. You also get the opportunity to work with line and staff managers in a collaborative way that will benefit all concerned.

2. Take risks. It's not enough to assume an innovative strategy or tactic can't be accomplished because there might be negative repercussions from one or more special interest groups (such as unions, employees, stockholders, management, or customers). Be creative and be willing to take calculated risks. For example, if you know management's credibility with employees is suffering, take the initiative to propose executive coaching and leadership training.

Despite the need to play a more strategic part, you can never lose sight of the traditional roles HR must continue to fulfill. You're the person management—from the CEO on down—turns to for such "hard" tasks as designing and implementing compensation and benefits programs to such "soft" skills as reading the mood of the workplace. There is also one more absolutely critical role you play.

The Conscience of Your Company

Values-based leadership became important to many companies in the late 1990s, when employee demand began to outstrip the supply, particularly in highly skilled and professional job markets. Many corporate leaders took a hard look at their organizations under the tutelage of Human Resources, began to rethink the mission and vision of their organizations, developing organizational values and publishing them. However, a shrinking economy and reduced profits led to layoffs and cutbacks, with pressure to increase production, sales, and, ultimately, profits.

Unfortunately, when times are tough, some leaders lose their focus on corporate values and on the importance of employees' morale and sense of self-worth. Ironically, many research studies show that the most successful companies are those that have strong corporate values their employees identify with and hold onto as their own. The worst time to lose focus on values is when a company needs to bolster its performance. That's when HR needs to lead the way.

Does your company need a values check? A question to ask that may identify whether a values review is necessary is this: "If the economy were to suddenly turn around and become an employees' market again, would we lose our best employees?" It's not a good situation if your employees are staying just because there's nothing better out there right now!

Ethics for the HR Professional

Perhaps the most critical aspect of business ethics for the one HR practitioner is the degree of integrity that you bring to your relationships with employees. Any questionable conduct on your part will not only set a poor example, but will cost you respect. Here are some of the most problematic areas for the HR professional who is balancing fairness and equality with business reality:

- **Hiring and Compensation.** Avoid any appearance of favoritism or discrimination. Always choose the best candidate as objectively as possible and decide merit raise percentages as carefully and fairly as possible within established procedures.

- **Discipline and discharge.** Discipline must be applied progressively and consistently. Never apply discipline to one employee but not another in similar circumstances. Document every step you take before discharging an employee.

- **Training and development.** Make sure opportunities for training and advancement are made available to all who desire and deserve them, not just a favored few.

- **Performance evaluations and promotions.** Avoid problems by making sure employees understand the performance evaluation process and then apply it precisely and fairly. Thoroughly document all evidence used to reach and support promotion decisions. Never let your personal feelings color the way certain employees are rated.

- **Employee privacy.** Keep compensation and raise information, use of leave time and employee assistance programs, and discipline actions in strictest confidence.

- **Discrimination.** Treat every employee with respect and dignity. Race, color, sex, religion, national origin, sexual orientation, physical condition, or appearance cannot be allowed to affect your hiring or employee decisions.

- **Favoritism and personal relationships.** Hiring a family member, promoting someone perceived to be a close personal friend, or dating an employee are all situations that put you at risk of charges of special treatment.

Why HR Matters

So why senior management should submit to a values check, give you a place at strategy sessions, and listen to your input? Because it makes good business sense, that's why! A study by consulting firm Watson Wyatt proves for the first time that there is a cause-and-effect relationship between HR practices and financial performance.

According to the firm's Human Capital Index," superior HR practices are not only correlated with improved financial returns but also tend to be a leading indicator of increased shareholder value. The year-long study found that companies with the best HR practices provided a 64 percent total return to shareholders (TRS) over a 5-year-period—more than three times the 21 percent TRS for companies with the weakest HR practices. That's a statistic that no bottom-line-oriented CEO can afford to ignore.

The survey also identified 43 specific HR practices that play the greatest role in creating shareholder value. According to the study, a significant improvement in all practices is associated with a 47 percent increase in market value. The 43 practices are divided into five key areas, and the research quantifies exactly how much an improvement in each area is expected to increase a company's market value:

- Total rewards and accountability: 16.5 percent
- Collegial, flexible workplace: 9 percent
- Recruiting and retention excellence: 7.9 percent
- Communications integrity: 7.1 percent
- Focused HR service technologies: 6.5 percent
- Total improvement from the above 47 percent

Other intriguing findings include the following:

- Making a stronger effort to link pay to performance, such as through stock programs, incentive/profit sharing plans, or higher pay for top performers, is associated with a 6.3 percent increase in market value overall.
- Capitalizing on basic communication technology leads to a 4.2 percent gain in market value.
- Companies that support flexible work arrangements, such as flextime, telecommuting, and job sharing, have 3.5 percent higher market value.

So there it is: Hire the right people, create an environment that supports creativity and productivity, and leverage technology—HR leads the way!

Leveraging HR

If you want to be a real partner in your company's business and have input into the strategic planning process, you need to leverage your position. One management expert believes that HR needs to adopt a "captain of the ship" approach. In other words, you need to assume responsibility for all people-related performance issues, as well as for the HR mainstays of pay and paperwork.

What Your CEO Really Wants to Know

How do you prove that HR deserves a place on the strategic management team? By proving to your CEO that your approach to

HR contributes to the company's growth and profitability and gives the organization a measurable advantage over your competitors.

Here is a list of questions that highly HR's strategic role. If you can answer these questions with certainty, you are a strategic partner. If you have difficulty with some of the questions, use those as goal-setting guidelines.

Staffing

- Do we attract and hire the very best people we can afford?
- Do we have the right number of people in our organization?
- Does having great employees really make a difference in our industry?
- Does HR have a metric system to ensure that the company is not overstaffed?
- Do we compare head count per unit of production or sales to that of our direct competitors to ensure that we don't have head count "fat"?
- Are we understaffed in areas where, if we added people in key areas, we would increase our profitability?

Productivity

- Are our people the most productive in the industry?
- Does HR have evidence that having the best employees is a critical success factor in our industry (because the most profitable firms have a high proportion of quality employees and less successful firms have a lower proportion of quality employees)?

Compensation

- Are we overpaying our employees for the output they produce?
- Can HR show the impact of pay increases? What is the percentage increase in employee performance as the result of every 1 percent increase in pay?

- Is there evidence that our benefits programs really attract or keep people?
- Is there evidence that our benefits programs really attract or keep people?

Training and Development

- Do we improve the people we have, making them more skilled and productive?
- What is the percent increase in performance as a result of every $1,000 spent on training?

Retention

- Do we retain our key and/or most productive people at a higher rate than our best competitors?
- Do we show that our voluntary turnover rate is lower than our competitors' for key executives, top performers, individuals with key competencies, and all individuals in hard-to-hire positions?

Performance Management

- Do we "fix" our problem employees rapidly or get rid of them if they are too expensive to fix?
- Should we get rid of poor performers who can't be fixed faster than our competitors?
- Is there evidence HR identifies and effectively fixes poor managers?

Return on Investment (ROI)

- Is there evidence HR is a major contributor (among overhead functions) to corporate success or profitability?
- Is HR efficient and continuously improving?
- Is the ROI in HR higher than the ROII for capital or for plant and equipment?

- What is our "people profit"—the number of dollars of personnel costs we must incur in order to generate a dollar of profit?

Leveraging Human Capital

- Do we forecast and prevent people problems better than the best in the industry?
- Do we rapidly redeploy our people resources from areas of low return in the corporation to areas of high return?
- What is our productivity (output) per dollar of "people costs" spent? (People costs include salary, benefits, training, HR department costs, etc.)
- Can HR show the productivity trend (past years' actual costs and future projections) compared to our chief competitors?

Employee Satisfaction

- Are our employees satisfied?
- Do employees report that they are more satisfied this year with the way they are treated (compared to last year)?
- Does HR have evidence of the impact of employee satisfaction on our employees' productivity and retention?

Strategy

- Is our overall HR strategy aligned with our business strategy?
- Is there evidence it adequately shifts as our business needs change?
- Has HR done a competitive analysis (overall and by function) to see where we need to shift our efforts in order to beat our competitors in every HR category?

On average, 60 percent of all corporate dollars are spent on people costs. That's why you need to be prepared to demonstrate and quantify how HR increases the company's compensative edge.

Selling HR

Just like buyers of your company's products or services, HR's customers (employees, supervisors, and management) respond favorably to good customer-service techniques. But to get the most out of your department, marketing and sales principles can be equally useful.

Do you think that sales and marketing are inconsistent with your customer-service responsibilities? If so, think of it this way: If your customers don't understand and enthusiastically buy into the services you're providing, you're wasting a lot of valuable time and resources, and your credibility is compromised.

Here are some strategies—courtesy of your colleagues in Sales and Marketing—that can help you create excitement and buy-in for your products and services:

- **1. Develop a referral strategy.** Employees aren't your only customers. Supervisors, managers, and executives are also your customers. It's not unusual to find that some of these customers may view HR as an adversary. Using the power of referrals and expectation agreements can change that. In sales, referrals represent the most predictable, perpetual, and profitable source of growing and expanding your business. Translated to the HR arena, one way to get reluctant managers on your team is to leverage your base of satisfied customers by developing a referral strategy.

- **2. Define your unique selling proposition.** Identify and communicate the most powerful features and benefits of your product and services clearly and succinctly.

- **3. Educate, and then follow up.** Your customers initially want to know only three things: (1) What is it?, (2) What will it do for me?, and (3) How much does it cost (e.g. time, effort, money)? The typical HR approach is to develop and distribute an information tool and conclude that the job is done until it has to be revised because of business strategy and/or federal, state, or local law changes. However, if your customers aren't satisfied, they won't come back—

and you need satisfied customers to successfully introduce and implement new initiatives. Providing customers with consistent, frequent, and useful information encourages them to come back for more.

- **4. Form strategic alliances.** Develop a personal strategy to host or promote others' agendas and get others to host or promote yours. This approach is particularly effective in organizations with multiple business operating units. HR can help facilitate strategic alliances that cut across the organization, offer win-win solutions for everyone, and make all your HR customers happy.

Become an HR MBA

One criticism of HR professionals has been that they lack business and financial acumen. So, do you need to have an MBA in order to be taken seriously as a strategic partner? No of course not. But you may need to start thinking more like a business person—especially since all the responsibility for running your corner of the business is on your shoulders.

In order to survive and excel in the future, you'll need to be able to:

- Understand your company's market and customers.
- Identify economic and competitive trends that can impact your company.
- Develop credible financial and staffing forecasts.
- Analyze and solve complex financial and budget problems.
- Help operating managers prepare valid budgets for HR-related services and resources, including talent acquisition.

Your functional management skills may also need to be expanded and refined. **Leveraging your role will require you to...**

- Complete projects on time and on budget.
- Provide more-effective insight and solutions to managing your talent.

- Give better advice and guidance with respect to functional and business performance measures.

- Manage multiple integrated projects.

- Become an HR services broker for needs such as talent acquisition, learning, professional development, etc.

Always Remember Your Customers

There is a lot you need to know to be successful at your job. If it all seems to be too much, remember how important you are to the people in your organization. A recent study looked at what makes some mergers a success when others, seemingly well thought-out, failed, came to a heartening conclusion: Companies that involved HR in the early stages of a merger or acquisition and use them as an expert resource throughout the entire process had successful outcomes.

The study found that HR is typically not significantly involved in a merger or acquisition until the integration planning and implementation stages. By failing to involve HR at the very earliest stages, companies are unable to plan and counteract the people issues and the related organizational and cultural issues that inevitably arise.

In successful mergers and acquisitions, HR professionals were substantially involved during the due diligence stage in 72 percent of the successful deals—and only 39 percent of those that failed. Once again, HR's value as a strategic partner is confirmed.

Job One: Learn Your Organization

One of the most important things you can do as a one HR practitioner is learn the organization you're in, from bottom to top and edge to edge. It takes time and effort. There are always obstacles in your path—fires to put out, paperwork to finish, and unexpected turns to event. If you want to make your job easier and also increase your stature in the company, you simply have to make time to understand what your organization does and how it does it.

Understand Your Starting Position

Although you are most likely—and understandably—anxious to make the job your own and implement your ideas, take a step back first. You can't improve on what's already in place unless you know where your staring point is.

An excellent exercise for the new, One HR Manager is to conduct an HR audit. This is basically an investigation of your organization's current practices, policies, and procedures. Here's a broad outline of what you need to do (a detailed discussion of auditing policies and procedures can be found in the next chapter that follows):

Take a comprehensive look at how your company handles:

- Benefits

  - Metrics
  - New-employee orientation
  - Perfomance management
  - Personnel files

  - Recruitment and retention
  - Safety and Health
  - Training

- **HR communications**

- **Compensation**

- **Legal compliance**

Create and implement an action plan addressing any inadequacies or mismatches that turned up in the audit. Here's an example of how you might go about auditing your organization's performance management system using metrics:

Metrics

Your basic metrics audit might include evaluations of the following areas depending on your organization:

- Turnover rate
- Turnover rate of top performers
- Absenteeism rate
- Cost per hire
- Cost-efficiency of benefits and training
- Analysis of exit interviews
- Pretax profit per employee

The results should be benchmarked against rates for other businesses in the same industry and in the geographic area to ensure that your compensation rates and other metrics are competitive. Metrics also need to be assessed for whether they appropriately support the company's business objectives.

Performance Management

In auditing performance management, you would need to look at:

- How performance evaluations are done (which can be a matter of how well supervisors are trained)
- How well discipline procedures are followed
- What percentage of employees are given measurable objectives for improvement
- Whether those objectives align with company business strategies
- What development plans are in place to retain high-potential employees and bring poor performers up to speed

Learn What Your Organization Does

Once you know all about the HR aspects of your new organization, it's time to really dig into what the rest of the organization does. What products do you make? What services do you perform? Who are your customers? How, exactly, does the work get done? Who are the players in your industry? Who are your biggest competitors? Who are your partners? You can't be a key strategic player if you don't understand how products get from point A to point B or how assignments are made and carried out.

For HR people to become strategic partners, they must understand bottom-line business issues. This means learning more about the specific objectives of your organization and also understanding the competitive environment and marketplace trends. After all, how can you begin to determine what competencies employees need if you don't know what business you're in? Here are some tips for finding out what you need to know about your new organization:

Want to Be Seen as a Strategic Player?
Know the Answers to These Questions

Are you familiar with the organization's marketing plans?

Is the organization meeting financial goals?

What is your organization doing to ensure a future market?

Have you read the past and current financial statements?

What is your markup percentage? Are you achieving it?

How do your costs compare with similar business costs?

Are you showing a good profit?

What percentage of sales do your labor costs comprise?

If you expand now, will you generate enough profit and cash flow to meet short-term cash needs?

If your sales are either up or down, can you explain why?

Is management meeting its performance goals?

Which product lines are the most profitable?

What is the depreciation schedule for plant and equipment?

How reliable are the organization's suppliers?

Are computer software and hardware installations efficient and up to date?

Is a quality program being implemented and followed?

Are inventory levels and turnover ratios within acceptable and targeted ranges?

Are productivity standards and goals established and followed?

Learn about Your Company's Products or Services

Perhaps you have always worked in a service organization and now are the HR person for a manufacturing plant, or perhaps you came from an engineering firm and now work in financial services. To be as effective as possible, you should give yourself a crash course in your new industry.

- Take an in-depth tour through your company's website or print catalogs and brochures. Read everything. Many companies have their mission and philosophy online, along with biographies of key personnel and histories of the company. Browse through the catalog. Educate yourself on all the full scope of products or services you offer.

- Use an online search engine to find your company's competitors. Browse their websites as well. In particular, look for information that describes their philosophy and mission. Take note of those in your geographic area. Perhaps their HR people are potential future contacts for you.

Now that you know what you do, find out how you do it.

Learn About People and Processes

There's no substitute for HRBWA. This is HR-speak for "Human Resources by Walking Around." It involves meeting employees and asking questions as you go. HRBWA is a surefire way to acquire knowledge about how your company gets its products and services out the door. Here are some stops to make on your "travel":

- Introduce yourself to managers and supervisors. Let them know you are genuinely interested in getting to know them and their people. Ask for their suggestions on the best way to do that. Ask who their key people are. Ask them when it would be a good time for you to visit with them and to get more information about what they do.

- Do a "shadowing" experience in each department, performing a range of jobs and "walking in the shoes" of salespeople, customer service reps, production line employees, and those in the warehouse. If it is impractical to actually perform a job, at least try to observe the mechanics of how the jobs get done.

- Attend department meetings. Regular staff meetings give you an opportunity to meet a lot of people in a short time, and also to learn about the inner workings of each department.

As you learn more about the company, you'll naturally absorb the lingo, acronyms, and insider terminology common to your organization. You'll be surprised at how quickly you'll be able to "talk the talk" after you take your walks!

Reach Out to Your Managers

Another "must do" is spending time to get to know the company's managers, bringing them on board to your agenda, and earning their respect. Why? Because the sweeping changes in today's workplace have significantly altered not only the role of HR, but the role of managers as well.

As a result of things as downsizing, reengineering, and self-directed work teams, there are fewer line managers to go around, and those who remain have much greater responsibility. They're managing more people and/or bigger projects, and they're being called on to make quicker business decisions.

These factors can work to your advantage. Managers are beginning to realize they need help with employee-relations problems as well as with general business issues. Line managers want HR to talk their language and help them meet the demands for productivity, cost control, and sales.

Remember that HR and line managers come from disparate cultures. Their training, experience, and objectives can be very different. HR comes from a background that is basically behaviorally based. Managers tend to be bottom-line oriented. As a result, HR is often seen as "soft," while the managers see themselves as working on the "hard" end of the business. HR often wants to talk about resolving conflict, whereas management wants to know how to raise market share or cut manufacturing costs. In addition, there are cultural differences that separate every corporate function. For example, Marketing differs from IT, and Sales is miles apart from Accounting.

How to Build Bridges

So what can HR do to build bridges across these cultural gaps? Your training helps you be a communications link between all departments, and is invaluable in helping you develop productive relationships with managers from every department.

- **Do the nuts and bolts of HR really well.** You need to do an excellent job managing day-to-day HR operations, because the first exposure many managers have to HR is when they have questions about policy and procedure. By proving your competence on routine HR issues, you'll increase the willingness of managers to consult you on larger business concerns.

- **Get rid of HR efforts that don't add value.** Once you know the business, you can analyze HR's contributions in terms of what it offers to the organization and whether all efforts meet organizational goals. The way to do this is by being willing to validate every HR efforts, from childcare centers to the employee newsletter, and get rid of those that don't show a return for your investment of time.

- **Develop relationships throughout the organization.** HR has a responsibility to cultivate relationships throughout the organization. Don't wait for managers to come to you with problems. Seek them out and learn about their business issues.

Get yourself invited to department meetings. Volunteer for task forces. Ask a manager's advice. Don't sit in the office and wait for the phone to ring!

- **Help managers become more confident in their HR roles.** It's HR role to train managers to be competent. You can't expect managers to have competency in areas such as interviewing, progressive discipline, and running staff meetings unless you train them. Provide managers with coaching and training in these skills. The more managers can help with the work of HR, the more valuable HR will become. Why? Because helping managers become more competent at routine HR tasks frees up your time for more strategic, value-added work.

- **Use their language.** Managers care more about outcomes than they do about rules. You need to be able to articulate your point of view using those terms. When you want to be heard in France, you speak French, don't you? Well, if you want to be heard among managers, you need to use terminology they understand.

- **Be flexible.** Although HR has to establish policies, rules, and procedures in an effort to create fairness, HR professionals need to understand that rules can and should be broken when an individual situation calls for it. Managers want HR to tailor solutions to their particular needs, not offer one-size-fits-all programs.

- **Focus on the same goals.** For managers to trust you, they have to know you're working toward the same objectives they are. This means focusing on bottom-line goals such as customer satisfaction, competitiveness, and profitability. How can you ensure that you're working toward the same things? Get involved in the business- planning process.

Communicate…again and again. HR staffers must talk, work, and communicate with managers on a regular basis. In theory, it sounds simple. In practice, this kind of regular contact is much harder to maintain.

Gain Employee Trust

It's not enough to get management on board with your program—you have to have the support of employees. Especially when starting in a new position, you may find that respect and/or trust for HR is lacking, for whatever reasons. Perhaps they have experienced limited access to HR, and haven't received timely or accurate responses to their HR questions in the past. Maybe there has been poor or even no communication about policies, benefits, pay, and so on. Perhaps the organization's policies have been misinterpreted or applied inconsistently by the former HR staff. If you find yourself in this situation, winning the respect of employees becomes a top priority.

The strategy for doing this is a familiar one: As I've said repeatedly in this section, you need to be a visible presence in the organization. Get out from behind your desk, get out on the floor, and observe, ask questions, and listen.

When you feel that you have a handle on the issues, start working on the solutions. Many of the strategies that will help you effectively partner with management also work for mending HR's relationship with employees.

- **Set customer-service benchmarks.** Resolve to answer questions within a certain time period: perhaps it's 2 hours, perhaps it's 24, but never ignore an employee call, question, or e-mail. Even if your answer is "I will have to research that and get back to you," make sure employees know that you have heard them and are interested in helping.

- **Use their language.** Remember that HR jargon may be meaningless to an employee. Worse, it may make the person feel that you are avoiding giving them a straight answer. When answering questions and explaining policies, always use the most clearly understandable language you can. Never send out a communication full of acronyms that are not fully defined or explained.

- **Be flexible.** Good judgment requires context. In spite of all your policies and procedures, you'll probably find that most situations have shades of gray that require careful thought and consideration. If you find yourself tempted to quote the policy book—stop! Make sure that employee knows that you are considering his or her individual circumstances.

- **Let employees know you have set goals for HR that put them first.** In every interaction, demonstrate by your words and actions that your one-person HR department is completely committed to their success and the success of the organization.

- **Communicate...again and again.** In the next section, you'll get tips and techniques for leveraging your HR communications to serve employees' needs.

Remember, it will take time and effort to track down specifics—and you'll most likely be fighting fires that come up on a daily basis and struggling to carve out time for auditing. And you may be thinking about what's waiting for you as you visit departments and attend staff meetings. But the information and insight you gain into your organization and its people will form the basis for all the actions that will follow.

CHAPTER TWO

THE PROCESS OF EMPLOYING AND MAINTAINING

The Employment Process

Employing people starts with the recognition that you need an employee and ends when the employee leaves your organization. Find information here on everything from recruiting, hiring, and orienting to training, policies, salary and benefits, performance management and improvement, and organization communication and culture. Find all of the basics about Human Resources.

The Human Resources function is served in an organization long before an HRF department is formed. Because paying employees starts out in accounting, usually an accounting and payroll clerk gets the nod. Recruiting, hiring, training, and all of the other HR functions are performed hit or miss with just about everyone in the organization doing a part of the role. But, as the organization grows, so, too, does the need for professional HR staff. Want to know more about Human Resources, the HR department, the HR function and more? You've stopped by the right door here.

When recruiting, selecting, staffing and hiring, pick the smartest person you can find. Retention of your best employees starts with your recruiting, staffing and hiring strategies, policies and procedures. Recruiting, testing, selection and staffing are the focus of these resources, from the determination of the need to fill a position until the onsite job interview.

Once posted, your job opening attracts many applicants. Selecting the best applicants for an interview sometimes feels like a crap shoot, but you can improve your chances of selecting qualified potential employees for interviews. These resources will help.

Conducting a Safe and Legal Interview

How to conduct a safe, legal interview that also enables you to select the best candidate for your open positions is important. The interview is one of the significant factors in hiring. Perhaps the traditional interview is accorded too much power in selection. Learn more interviewing tips and interviewing techniques to make your interviews a power tool and process to evaluate candidates.

Job searching specialists and career counselors recommend that job applicants write a customized resume cover letter to company each resume sent to an employer. They're right. As an employer, a customized resume cover letter matters.

A resume cover letter saves you time, connects the candidate's relevant experience to your advertised job, and provides insight into the candidate's skills, characteristics, and experience. The factors viewed as important by your candidate are emphasized in a resume cover letter.

What to look for in a Resume Cover Letter

The resume cover letter enhances the resume and should not be sent to you as a stand-alone document. You are looking for a well-written, informative resume cover letter that demonstrates the candidate's attention to detail. Appropriate grammar and correct spelling tell you that the candidate invested the time and energy to make a positive impression.

Typos and poor formatting in a resume cover letter, on the other hand, signal an applicant that failed to take the time to make a good impression. Employers rightly regard the resume cover letter as their best example of the candidate's ability to express thoughts in writing. This is because the average applicant's resume cover letter is not reviewed whereas most candidates ask multiple people to review their resume.

Some tips you might like to consider using when reading through a resume cover letter:

- Determine the position for which the candidate is applying. (This should be in the first sentence, but if your experience is anything like mine, many candidates don't specify a position. They write statements such as, "I saw your ad on the FootPrint News Paper and think my background and experience are a perfect match for it.") The candidate should not make you guess.

- Look for an overall statement about why the candidate is applying for your advertised job.

- If your job ad or job posting stated specific skills, experiences, and traits, the candidate should have summarized why and how their specific skills, experiences, and traits match what you are seeking.

- The candidate's summary should provide specific examples that support the fact that their specific skills, experiences, and traits actually are a match for what you seek.

- Look for an action-oriented ending to the resume cover letter that expresses the candidate's hoped for conclusion. "I look forward to an interview during which we can further explore the specifics of my potential match with your advertised position."

- Some job search professionals suggest that candidates state that they will call the employer to follow up. This is a nightmare in a small-to- mid-sized company in that 100 or more resumes are often received for a single advertised position. Maybe larger companies have recruiting staff members who can field the phone calls, but smaller companies certainly don't. In fact, human resources professionals have a name for job searchers who call repeatedly—they call them stalkers.

As an employer of choice, you can save your candidates' time and worry. Send a post card or letter acknowledging receipt of their application. The note can simply state that their application has been received, and if they are one of the people whose qualifications seem to most closely match your needs, you will call them to schedule an interview.

- Once you have reviewed the resume, look back at the resume cover letter for explanations of any items that are unusual on the resume. This may include an explanation for a gap in the candidate's employment history.

Your candidate might explain why they have changed employers twice in two years, as another example. The letter might state that the candidate's expected graduation date is June. If oddities in the candidate's employment history are not explained to your satisfaction on either the resume or in the resume cover letter, you're probably smart to pass on interviewing the candidate.

Candidates who fail to spend the time to construct an effective resume cover letter deserve less attention than candidates who understand the resume cover letter's importance—and write one. These tips summarize the key knowledge you can gain from an effective resume cover letter.

Employee Management
(The Human Management Concerns)

Whether you're in Human Resources or line management, you'll find how to, theoretical and even, inspirational information about employee management, supervision and leadership within these resources. Looking for input to further develop your own employee management and leadership skills? Seeking insight into working well with other managers and leaders? You'll find the information you need here.

Employee management is your first concern if you are a supervisor or manager at work. Effective management of employees allows you to accomplish your goals at work. Effective employee management allows you to capitalize on the strengths of other employees and their ability to contribute to the accomplishment of work. Successful employee management helps employee motivation, employee development, and employee retention.

Human Resource Management (HRM) is the function within an organization that focuses on recruitment of, management of, and providing direction for the people who work in the organization. Human Resource Management can also be performed by line managers.

Human Resource Management is the organizational function that deals issues related to people such as compensation, hiring, performance management, organization development, safety, wellness, benefits, employee motivation, communication, administration, and training.

Even the best organizations periodically make mistakes in dealing with people. They mess up their opportunity to create effective, successful, positive employee relations.

They treat people like children and then ask why people fail so frequently to live up to their expectations. Managers apply different rules to different employees and wonder why workplace negativity is so high. People work hard and infrequently receive positive feedback.

At the same time, many organizations invest untold energy in actions that ensure employees are unhappy. They ensure ineffective employee relations results. As an example, one of the most important current trends in organizations is increasing employee involvement and input. Organizations must find ways to utilize all of the strengths of the people they employ. Or, people will leave to find work in an organization that does.

- Teamwork in Workplaces

Workplaces need to recruit new populations and non-traditional employees. And, workplaces urgently need to retain valued employees. The book **High Five**, by Ken Blanchard and Sheldon Bowles talks about building powerfully effective teams. The book emphasizes that *"the essence of a team,* "according to Dr. Blanchard, is "the genuine understanding that none of us is as smart as all of us." Teams allow people to achieve things far beyond our own individual ability. But teamwork also requires powerful motivation for people to put the good of the group ahead of their own self-interest.

One thing I observed about business organizations is that, despite they have all what they need they often fail to:

- Retain valued employees
- Develop empowered people working together to serve the best interests of the organization, and

- Create an environment in which each employee contributes all of their talents and skills to the success of organizational goals.

The next time you are confronted with any of the following proposed actions, ask yourself this question. Is the action likely to create the result, for powerfully motivating employee relations, that you want to create?

The following are twenty mistakes employers often make

Below are twenty mistakes organizations make to mess up their relationships with the people they employ. As a Human Resource Manager, it is very important to avoid these employee relations nightmares. As you continue to read and understand these unwanted scenarios, you will realize that they are very common and need to be addressed before they get off hand. They are also simple to grasp:

- Add another level of hierarchy because people are not doing what you want them to do. (More watchers get results!)

- Appraise the performance of individuals and provide bonuses for the performance of individuals and complain that you cannot get your staff working as a team.

- Add inspectors and multiple audits because you don't trust people's work to meet standards.

- Fail to create standards and give people clear expectations so they know what they are supposed to do, and wonder why they fail.

- Create hierarchical, permission steps and other roadblocks that teach people quickly their ideas are subject to veto and wonder why no one has any suggestions for improvement. (Make people beg for money!)

- Ask people for their opinions, ideas, and continuous improvement suggestions, and fail to implement their suggestions or empower them to do so. Better. Don't even provide feedback about whether the idea was considered.

- Make a decision and then ask people for their input as if their feedback mattered.

- Find a few people breaking rules and company policies and chide everybody at company meetings rather than dealing directly with the rule breakers. Better? Make everyone wonder "Who" the bad guy is.

- Make up new rules for everyone to follow as a means to address the failings of a few.

- Provide recognition in expected patterns so that what started as a great idea quickly becomes entitlement. (As an example, buy Friday lunch when production goals are met. Wait until people start asking you for the money if they cannot attend the lunch!)

- Treat people as if they are untrustworthy—watch them, track them, admonish them for every slight failing—because a few people are untrustworthy.

- Fail to address behavior and actions of people that are inconsistent with stated and published organizational expectations and policies. (Better yet, let non-conformance go on until you are out of patience; then ambush the next offender with a disciplinary action).

- When managers complain they cannot get to all of their reviews because they have too many directly reporting staff members, hire more supervisors to do reviews. (Fail to recognize that an hour per quarter per person invested in development is the manager's most important job.)

- Create policies for every contingency, thus allowing every little management latitude in addressing individual employee needs.

- Conversely, have so few policies, that employees feel as if they reside in a free-for-all environment of favoritism and unfair treatment.

- Make every task a priority. People will soon believe there are no priorities. More importantly, they will never feel as if they have accomplished a complete task or goal.

- Schedule daily emergencies that prove to be false. This will ensure employees don't know what to do, or are, minimally, jaded about responding when you have a true customer emergency.

- Ask employees to change the way they are doing something without providing a picture of what you are attempting to accomplish with the change. Label them "resisters" and send them to change management training when they don't immediately hop on the train.

- Expect that people learn by doing everything perfectly the first time rather than recognizing that learning occurs most frequently in failure.

- Letting a person fail when you had information that he did not, which he might have used to make a different decision.

It is often said that human resource planning is the process by which a management determines how an organization should move from its current manpowered position to its desired manpower position. Very often this way a management strives to have the right number and the right kind of people at the right places at the right time.

Human resource planning consists of a series of activities:

1. Forecasting future manpower requirements

2. Making an inventory of present manpower resources.

3. Anticipating manpower problems by projecting present resources into the future.

4. Planning the necessary programs of requirement, selection, training and development to ensure that future manpower requirements are properly met.

Human Resource Planning is necessary for one or more of the following reasons:

1. Effective manpower planning is required for every organization to carry on the work efficiently.

2. There is a constant need for replacing personnel who have grown old or who retire so that the work doesn't suffer.

3. Human Resource Planning is essential because of frequent labor turnover that arises from social and economical factors like voluntary quits, marriage, promotions, etc.

4. Due to rising standards of living large quantities of goods are require because of which human resource planning is unavoidable.

5. The present workforce has to be changed in relation to the challenging needs of technology and production.

6. Manpower planning is needed in order to identify areas of surplus personnel or tutoring.

Process of Human Resource Planning

1. Deciding goals or objectives

2. Estimating future organizational structure and manpower requirements

3. Auditing Human Resources

4. Planning job requirements and job descriptions

5. Developing a human resource plan.

Changing the tradition of your company

Changing your organizational culture is the toughest task you will ever take on. Your organizational culture was formed over years of interaction between the participants in the organization. Changing the accepted organizational culture can feel like rolling rocks uphill.

Organizational culture grows over the time. People are comfortable with the current organizational culture. For people to consider culture change, usually a significant event must occur. An event that rocks their world such as flirting with bankruptcy, a significant loss of sales and customers, or losing a million dollars, might get people's attention.

Even then, to recognize that the organizational culture is the culprit and to take steps to change it, is a tough journey. In no way do I mean to trivialize the difficulty of the experience of organizational culture change by summarizing it in this article, but here are my best ideas about culture change that can help your organization grow and transform.

When people in an organization realize and recognize that their current organizational culture needs to transform to support the organization's success and progress, change can occur. But change is not pretty and change is not easy.

The good news? Organizational culture change is possible. Culture change requires understanding, commitment, and tools.

Steps in Organizational Culture Change

There are three major steps involved in changing an organization's culture.

1. Before an organization can change its culture, it must first understand the current culture, or the way things are now. Do take the time to pursue the activities in this

2. Once you understand your current organizational culture, your organization must then decide where it wants to go, define its strategic direction, and decide what the organizational culture should look like to support success. What vision does the organization have for its future and how must the culture change to support the accomplishment of the vision?

3. Finally, the individuals in the organization must decide to change their behavior to create the desired organizational culture. This is the hardest step in culture change.

Plan the Desired Organizational Culture

The organization must plan where it wants to go before trying to make any changes in the organizational culture. With a clear picture of where the organization is currently, the organization can plan where it wants to be next.

Mission, vision, and values: to provide a framework for the assessment and evaluation of the current organizational culture, your organization needs to develop a picture of its desired future. What does the organization want to create for the future? Mission, vision, and values should be examined for both the strategic and the value based components of the organization. Your management team needs to answer questions such as:

- What are the five most important values you would like to see represented in your organizational culture?

- Are there values compatible with your current organizational culture? Do they exist now? If not, why not? If they are so important, why are you not attaining these values?

Take a look at the rest of the actions you need to take to change your organizational culture.

First of all, let us look at the following before coiling the entire values into perspectives.

- **What needs to happen to create the culture desired by the organization?** You cannot change the organizational culture without knowing where your organization wants to be or what elements of the current organizational culture need to change. What cultural elements support the success of your organization, or not? As an example, your team decides that you spend too much time agreeing with each other rather than challenging the forecasts and assumptions of fellow team members, that typically have been incorrect.

In a second example, your key management team members, who must lead the company, spend most of their time team building with various members of the team on an individual basis, and to promote individual agendas, to the detriment of the cohesive functioning of the whole group. Third, your company employees appear to make a decision, but, in truth, are waiting for the "blessing" from the company owner or founder to actually move forward with the plan.

However, knowing what the desired organizational culture looks like is not enough. Organizations must create plans to ensure that the desired organizational culture becomes a reality.

Change the Organizational Culture

It is more difficult of an existing organization than to create a culture in a brand new organization. When an organizational culture is already established, people must unlearn the old values, assumptions, and behaviors before they can learn the new ones.

The two most important elements for creating organizational cultural change are executive support and training.

- **Executive Support:** Executives in the organization must support the cultural change, and in ways beyond verbal support. They must show behavioral support for the cultural change. Executives must lead the change by changing their own behaviors. It is extremely important for executives to consistently support the change.

- **Training:** Culture change depends on behavior change. Members of the organization must clearly understand what is expected of them, and must know how to actually do the new behaviors, once they have been defined. Training can be very useful in both communicating expectations and teaching new behaviors.

Additional Ways to Change the Organizational Culture

Other components important in changing the culture of an organization are;

- **Create value and belief statements:** use employee focus groups, by department, to put the mission, vision, and values into words that state their impact on each employee's job. For one job, the employee stated; "I live the value of quality patient care by listening attentively whenever a patient speaks." This exercise gives all employees a common understanding of the desired culture that actually reflects the actions they must commit to on their jobs.

- **Practice effective communication:** keeping all employees informed about the organizational culture change process ensures commitment and success. Telling employees what is expected of them is critical for effective organizational culture change.

- **Review organizational structure:** changing the physical structure of the company to align it with the desired organizational culture may be necessary. As an example, in a small company, four distinct business units competing for product, customers, and internal support resources, may not support the creation of an effective organizational culture. These units are unlikely to align to support the overall success of the business.

Redesign your approach to rewards and recognition: you will likely need to change the reward system to encourage the behaviors vital to the desired organizational culture.

- **Review all work systems:** such as employee promotions, pay practices, performance management, and employee selection to make sure they are aligned with the desired culture. As an example, you cannot just reward individual performance if the requirements of your organizational culture specify teamwork. An executive's total bonus cannot reward the accomplishment of his department's goals without recognizing the importance of him playing well with others on the executive team to accomplish your organizational goals.

Leadership and Sponsorship in Action

If you work in an organization, you've heard this complaint repeatedly. Leaders and managers say they want change and continuous improvement but their actions do not match their words. The leaders' exhortations to employees ring false when their subsequent actions contradict their words. A CEO once asked me, "Why do they do what I do and not what I tell them to do?" Another asked, "Do I really have to change, too?" These are scary questions coming from leaders.

The power of an organization's leaders in creating the organization's values, environment, culture and actions is immeasurable. What to know how to "walk the talk" to enable organization change and improvement? Want to take the power away from the oft-repeated employee complaint that managers don't walk their talk? Start here to learn how to walk your talk. Or, use these ideas to help your organization's leaders and managers walk theirs. It's the shortest journey to empower change and the work environment they desire.

What you need to know about walking your talk

The most important tip comes first. If you do this first action well, the rest will follow more naturally. If the ideas you are promoting are congruent with your core beliefs and values, these actions will come easily, too. So, start with a deep understanding of "why" you want to see the change or improvement. Make certain it is congruent with what you deeply believe. Then, understand and follow these guidelines.

- Model the behavior you want to see from others. There is nothing more powerful for employees than observing the "big bosses" do the actions or behaviors they are requesting from others. As Mahatma Gandhi said, "Become the change you wish to see in the world." And, it will happen.

- If you make a rule or design a process, follow it, until you decide to change it. Why would employees follow the rules if the rule makers don't?

- Act as if you are part of the team, not always the head of it. Dig in and do actual work, too. People will appreciate that you are personally knowledgeable about the effort needed to get the work done. They will trust your leadership because you have undergone their experience.

- Help people achieve the goals that are important to them, as well as the goals that are important to you. Make sure there is something for each of you that will result from the effort and work.

- Do what you say you're going to do. Don't make rash promises that you can't keep. People want to trust you and your leadership.

- Build commitment to your organization's big goal. (You do have a big, overarching goal, don't you? Other than to make money, why does your organization exist?

- Use every possible communication tool to build commitment and support for the big goal, your organization's values and the culture you want to create. This includes what you discuss at meetings, in your corporate blog, on your Intranet, and so forth.

- Hold strategic conversations with people so people are clear about expectations and direction. Gerard Kleisterlee, Philips' president, is hold strategic conversations with as many groups as he can. "In order to build internal confidence, stimulate cross-boundary cooperation, and spark new product speed to market, Kleisterlee is sponsoring what he calls 'strategic conversations': dialogues that center around a focused set of themes that Kleisterlee believes will define Philips' future.

- Ask senior managers to police themselves. They must provide feedback to each other when they fail to walk their talk. It is not up to the second level managers and other employees to point out inconsistency. (Confronting a manager takes courage, facts and a broad understanding of the organization.) Senior managers must be accountable to each other for their own behavior.

In 1513, Machiavelli wrote, "There is nothing more difficult to plan, more doubtful of success, nor more dangerous to manage than the creation of a new system. For the initiator has the enmity of all who would profit by the preservation of the old system and merely lukewarm defenders in those who would gain by the new one."

Given these thoughts from Machiavelli—true for centuries—provide leadership and sponsorship through walking your talk. Incorporate these tips and behaviors to ensure the success of your organization. Walk your talk.

CHAPTER THREE

STRATEGIC HUMAN RESOURCE PLANNING AND DEVELOPMENT

How to Get Your Priorities Straight

As personnel of a Human Resources department of one, your success will stem from your ability to plan effectively for your organization's short- term, midrange, and long-term priorities. This chapter is packed with information on all the critical HR areas that factor into your department's strategic plan.

Not surprisingly, people-related issues will most likely be your top priority. In fact, when 200 senior executives were asked to choose their companies' top strategic priorities, respondents chose workforce-related priorities as four of their top five:

1. Attracting and retaining skilled staff

2. Changing organizational culture and employee attitudes

3. Changing leadership and management behaviors

4. Improving workforce performance

Chances are, one or more of these is also on your CEO's radar screen. To be an effective partner with management, your strategic plan needs to address these priorities. If people are your greatest competitive asset, then you need to be sure your organization is a place where they can grow and thrive.

Strategic Planning Defined

According to the International Public Management Association for Human Resources, strategic planning determines where an organization is going over the next several years, how it's going to get there, and how it will know if it got there or not. With your strategic plan, you are committing to paper a definition of your department of your department's goals and the steps you will take to achieve those goals. Much of your time is taken up with administrative tasks, and without a strategic plan, you may end up pushing paper and putting out fires, but find yourself outside the management loop, with no idea of where you should be a year from now.

Strategic planning, at its most basic, is really nothing more than setting specific, measurable goals and then committing to a timetable and a plan of action for meeting those goals. The strategic part is choosing goals that align with the goals of your organization.

The Strategic Planning Process

When senior managers undertake a strategic analysis, they look both inside the company and outside it to identify strengths, weaknesses, problems, challenges, and opportunities. Typically, here is what will happen:

- They will compare the organization's performance against the standards set the previous year, and also against competitors' performances and industry standards.

- They will look at issues unique to their company and those that are faced across the board, and assess how the organization fared.

- They will attempt to honestly assess where there are problems affecting the organization's performance.

- They will follow these steps for both the organization as a whole and for individual departments and/or divisions.

- After this is done and the facts are gathered and analyzed, they will set goals and priorities for the company as a whole.

- Managers will set priorities for their departments and/or divisions that tie directly back to the main business strategy for the coming year.

Being part of the team that conducts this analysis is a sure sign you are seen as a strategic player. However, what should you do if you are not yet seen in that light, or if your organization is more laissez-faire about planning? In that case, doing your own strategic planning is your entry point.

- Ask for a meeting with your boss to discuss the company's plans for next year.

- Before the meeting, do your own strategic analysis of your department and also of what you have observed of other departments and of the organization as a whole.

- Be prepared with a list of what you see as strengths, weaknesses, and priorities. Discuss the goals you would like to set for your department and ask for feedback on how those goals align with the company's goals.

- Make sure you have budget requests and estimates for new initiatives and top priorities.

Choosing Your Top Priorities

With so many priorities, how can you choose where to focus your strategic-planning efforts? Here are just a few of the major areas your HR colleagues are putting at the top of their goals:

- Finding innovative and cost-effective solutions to people issues. Organizations need more than ever to pay close attention to the bottom line. As a large portion of any company's expenses is related to personnel, HR is playing a more strategic and prominent role in decisions on all people issues.

- Implementing staff reductions and other cost-containment initiatives. If companies lay off employees, leave positions unfilled, and make other cost reductions to try and stay profitable, it is up to HR to implement the reductions, assist terminated employees, and keep the retained workforce motivated and content. HR is also being asked to contribute ideas on how the company can continue to minimize expenses.

- Containing the cost of healthcare benefits. The exploding cost of health insurance in the United States threatens profitability. Yet it's important for companies to continue to offer attractive benefits packages, including good healthcare coverage, if they are to retain and attract the talent they need. However, HR is charged with finding the balance between helping the company minimize expenses and offering good benefits.

- Integrating new technology. HR is being charged with making better use of the Internet and intranets to store, organize, and disseminate information to employees, as well as with implementing self-service technology to reduce costs.

In the sections that follow, you will be introduced to all of the components that will factor into your day-to-day mission as well as into your periodic strategic planning.

HR Communications

Communication with employees is vital to your HR function. In fact, effective communication from HR is so important to your organization that the following information is just an introduction. Many of the sections that follow include specific communication strategies for such subjects as benefits, recruiting, and performance management. For now, we are just going to offer a brief overview of the most effective ways that HR professionals communicate the company's objectives and policies.

Handbooks and Manuals

The employee handbook is the master document of company policy and procedure. It is the most commonly used tool to communicate important information. It provides employees with guidance about wages, benefits, vacations, and a host of other workplace concerns, such as dress codes. The employee handbook also helps influence the company culture, and it sets the tone for the relationship between managers and employees.

The management policy manual is another excellent communication tool. The policy manual is a document for managers and supervisors only. While some issues may be covered in both documents, many topics found in the policy manual are not included in the handbook. For instance, management issues such as recruiting and evaluating employee performance will generally be found only in the management policy manual.

Note of Caution: Many countries' courts have found that certain wording in handbooks and manuals can create binding employment contracts. So if employers do not follow their written policies and procedures, they could be inviting lawsuits. You might consider including disclaimer statements explicitly informing employees that the information contained within is not intended as an employment contract.

Posters—in the United States of America

There are specific types of HR information, including compensation, nondiscrimination, and equal employment opportunity, that legally must be posted for all employees, such as a notice of the federal Fair Labor Standards Act, Family and Medical Leave Act, Uniformed Services Employment and Reemployment Rights Act, Employee Polygraph Protection Act, federal Minimum Wage, and Occupational Safety and Health Act, among others. There are additional posting requirements for federal contractors. Individual states in the United States may also have their own posting requirements. Posters are available through your local offices of the U.S. Department of Labor (DOL), Equal Employment Opportunity Commission (EECOC), and your state Department of Labor.

Bulletin Boards—
America and other countries in the world

To be effective, bulletin boards must be placed in prominent high-traffic areas where all employees will see them. Your company may need only one board for all employees, or perhaps one in each department. You can protect important HR posters by placing them under plastic or glass.

Employee Newsletters—
Western and European countries

Published monthly or, more typically, quarterly, employee newsletters are a popular way to convey information. You can announce new policies, benefit changes, job openings, business issues, service anniversaries, employee awards, and community activities. You can also use newsletters to promote awareness of governmental regulations and legislation affecting company business.

An employee newsletter can be a heavy responsibility for a single practitioner. It can also be an expensive proposition if it is professionally printed. Think carefully before starting one and consider alternatives, including the electronic options discussed in this section.

E-Mail and Intranet

E-mail and a company intranet are two of the most effective—and time efficient—means of communicating. E-mail can help you alert employees to new policies and procedures, remind them of corporate events, and share good news. By using e-mail, you can document when people receive and read messages and electronically file messages to retrieve when needed. If you are determined to publish a monthly newsletter, but lack the time and resources, an e-mailed "newsletter" just might be the solution.

If you have a company intranet, employees can access all kinds of HR, safety, and benefits information. All your policies, procedures, forms, benefits handouts, wellness messages, etc., can be digitalized and posted. Intranets make it possible to communicate with employees 24/7 and are excellent tools for organizations that have more than one shift and/or run 7- day operations.

Typically, intranets are protected by passwords and firewalls so that only employees can access information. Parts of the intranet can be reserved for even more-restricted access. With a corporate intranet, there are almost limitless possibilities for how you can communicate with employees.

Meetings
Group Meetings

Nothing is more effective than group presentations to ensure that everyone receives the same message and that it is not tainted by rumor or secondhand interpretation. Group meetings can be called to communicate information, both good and bad; introduce benefits changes; or announce new corporate initiatives. If your company is small enough, gathering everyone together is a way to build camaraderie.

Training Meetings

Almost every company has to run some training meetings. You may need to train managers and supervisors on a new performance appraisal system or conduct mandated sexual harassment training. Supervisors may need to hold safety training meetings or sales kickoff meetings with their groups. Even if you are not the person who will run the meeting, be sure managers and team leaders know you are available and able to help them create an agenda, gather necessary audiovisual and other equipment, review their presentations, and so on. If possible, sit in on such meetings so you know what employees are being told.

One-on-One Meetings

The life of an HR practitioner is filled with one-on-one meetings. For instance, you may need to meet with a supervisor who needs advice on a personnel problem you and/or supervisor can confirm that employees understand policy and procedure with one-on-one meetings. Some one-on- one meetings will be formally scheduled, but you will probably find that people will seek you out if you set aside time for "open" office hours to answer questions.

Orientation

The most important meeting at which to communicate HR policy is the new-employee orientation meeting. Orientation can be accomplished in a comprehensive one-on-one session on the employee's first day or worked into group sessions during initial job training. Most likely, employees will be required to make several important decisions about compensation and benefits soon after starting new jobs. Your orientation can help them make the best decisions.

You may wish to divide your orientation into two parts: company information provided by HR and job or departmental information provided by supervisors. If supervisors are responsible for this information, you can assist them by providing necessary materials and giving them tips on how to present it.

Open-Door Policy

If employees have questions or complaints, they should feel they can come to you for information. Consider establishing an open-door policy, or at least, set open hours when you will be available.

Getting the Message Delivered

Because different employees prefer different modes of communication, you may want to put your messages through two, three, or even more channels. For example, the new corporate benefits policy could be communicated in all of these ways, helping to ensure that every employee gets the message:

- E-mailed to all employees
- Posted on the company intranet
- Distributed through flyers placed in highly traveled areas
- Discussed at an all-employee meeting

Setting and Communicating Company Standards

Organizations set standards to serve the company's mission and corporate culture. If employees are to play their role of adhering to the goals and objectives that support the mission, they need to buy in to the mission. That's where you come in. You need to help management develop and communicate clear, easily understood standards that:

- Express basic expectations of employer performance and behavior
- Are uniform
- Apply to all workers at all times
- Are ongoing, not reserved for special circumstances

Through its standards, your company clarifies the basic expectations it has for employees. Managers have guidelines by which to monitor and manage performance. Communication is enhanced because everyone throughout the organization is one the same page. Also, fair and consistently applied standards can be a strong defense against legal claims of unfair performance appraisals, discrimination, favoritism, and the like.

Communicating Company News

Single HR practitioners may be called upon by management to deliver company news—both good and bad—to employees and sometimes, to the public. Typically subjects of such communications include information about layoffs, lawsuits, and negative attention from government agencies.

The first communication task is to determine, in consultation with management, whether your company's newsworthy event calls for a proactive response. In some cases, you're better off remaining silent. Let's say DOL delivers a negative audit of your wage-and-hour practices, or the Equal Employment Opportunity Commission (EEOC) files suit against you for race discrimination. In such cases, it's wise to wait until you have not only completed your review and analysis of the event but also been specifically asked about the situation or called on to address a rumor within the organization.

When formulating the company's response, whether proactive or reactive, think through the basic messages that should be conveyed, and:

- Limit your message to (ideally) no more than three main points directed to your audience (i.e., employees and/or customers).

- Prepare answers to anticipated follow-up questions. There may be details that should not be shared when answering other questions.

- If appropriate, review communications with legal counsel before the fact.

- Treat others with respect, even if they're adversaries. Individuals or organizations that are disrespectful are usually viewed negatively.

Budgeting and Resource Allocation

Planning and budgeting are critical functions and knowing how to put together a good budget empowers you and strengthens your strategic role. If you have already worked with budgets and budgeting, you are ahead of the game. But if you haven't, all is not lost. What follows is a very simple process for creating a budget.

Overview

Basically, a budget is a written document describing what you are going to do to accomplish your departmental goals. It outlines the money you will spend and when you will spend it. Of course, you need to balance your departmental needs and your budget numbers with the overall goals and available funds of your organization.

Your numbers will be (or should be) reviewed carefully by your accounting of finance department, so creating an accurate and workable plan gives your budget a better chance of being approved.

The accounting department will usually create account codes for each of your line items and assign them in their computer system. Every time money is approved or spent, they will track that event and take from the money allocated in your budget and show it as actually spent. Be advised, most organizations measure an individual's performance, at least in part, on how they manage their budget.

The budget you put together will ultimately become part of the larger corporate budget—but probably not until you participate in a series of discussions and meetings with upper management. Be patient with this process. Keep in mind that every department in the organization is competing for a limited poor of resources, so you will need to be prepared to back up your budgetary requests with a solid rationale and some concrete facts and figures to substantiate your need.

The Building Blocks

Two basic building blocks are required to create a budget. The first building block is constructed from the budget numbers from a prior year or years. You'll need to take that information and consider whether that number will increase or decrease based on your current and future needs. Your second building block is composed of your new budgetary requests.

If you are starting from scratch and don't have accurate information about the prior year, or if you know that the coming year is going to be substantially different, you'll need to start by developing a comprehensive month-by-month plan of your proposed activities for the year. You'll want to consider any new projects or agendas that you'll be undertaking.

For example, let's say that you discover that before you came aboard, there had never been a budget for outsourcing any HR functions. You decide you can save the company money by outsourcing payroll. You will need to carefully explore the costs of outsourcing and discuss this idea with management to get initial buy-in before you start your budgeting. Once that approval is obtained, you are going to have to do some serious homework to arrive at your proposed budget numbers.

You will need to demonstrate that you have shopped around for the best provider, have chosen the best provider, and that your expense will provide a good return on investment. Be prepared with figures that compare the costs of hiring personnel to the cost of outsourcing. Also be prepared to demonstrate that the move will ensure accuracy and free up the HR department to focus on the higher-level tasks.

Step 1: Put Together Your Figures

List all the anticipated expenses from your department, including such items as fees for recruitment, fringe benefits, regular salaries, bonuses, airfare, and projected costs of compensated leave. Then refer to the previous year's expenses and put a realistic new figure against each expense.

If you are involved in employment planning, this will involve creating a realistic budget based on projections for new employees and compensation. Part of the process will include analyzing hiring costs. Your analysis should include the cost of:

- Advertising
- Salaries of any recruiters

- Hours spent interviewing, testing, and training new employees
- Any temporary workers hired while filling the position
- The salary and benefits paid to the new employee compared to those of the one you are replacing.

When gathering data about last year's expenses, you may find that departmental records are not always well kept. Get whatever information you can from the Accounting or Finance Department about the expenses for the past financial year during the months in which these expenses have accrued. This will give you an idea about the nature and magnitude of expenses. If you still don't have sufficient information to make an informed decision, check with a colleague at a similar organization, or see if a local HR association can help. In the absence of concrete information, you may need to make a thoughtful estimate.

Before you begin to put your budget in a format, discuss this process with your accounting manager or whoever oversees the company's financials. Find out exactly what format he or she wants. For example, labor costs could be budgeted by each department or put completely under your HR budget. Office expenses could be totally under your budget, or they might be divided into different categories. Supplies might be in Purchasing's budget and mailing costs might be in the Operations' budget.

And here's something to consider: Just because it was in last year's budget doesn't mean it has to stay in this year's. Think carefully about your programs and projects. Are they worth the money and the investment in time? For example, just because your company has always participated in the local college/university job fair docsn't mean you have to continue the practice. Is it worth the expense in materials, booth rental, and time spent out of the office? What is the direct benefit to the company? How many people are recruited each year? What's the worst thing that could happen if you don't attend? By asking the hard questions, you may end up freeing that money for much-needed temporary services during benefits enrollment time.

Probably one of the best things you can do for yourself to simplify budget preparation is to learn and master—a spreadsheet program.

A spreadsheet program will take care of the mechanics of addition, subtraction, and simple percentage increases.

Step 2: Anticipate Future Needs

When estimating future needs, arrive at the best figure possible that is based on good information, your own experience, and accurate calculations. If you're smart, you'll set up a system for keeping accurate budget records to ease your preparation for next year. If you start working regularly with spreadsheets, you'll see that you can attach notes to the various cells. That way, when you sit down to make your next budget, you'll know why you spent money, where you ran short, and why you need more. It's also good to review your current budget on a monthly basis to see where you stand.

Step 3: Make Sure Your Budget Is Logical

Use this quick list to reality-check your initial budget:

- **Does it make sense?** Do the numbers look right? Are you comfortable with these numbers? If not, then get someone's opinion or rethink it yourself.

- **Does it add up?** Even if you use a computerized spreadsheet, you'll want to check your numbers. It's possible to make an error when devising the formulas for the individual cells.

- **Are the big items right?** Pay extra attention to the line items with higher figures, or where there are large increases from prior year budgets.

Step 4: Prepare Your Budgetary Assumption Document

Your budget is more than just numbers. Certain assumptions are built into it based on your research and reasoning. If you prepare a simple one—or two-page document compiling all your information, you and others can refer to it at budget review time. If there are errors in your budget, you'll want to be able to trace the source of your mistakes. Armed with a budget assumption document, you'll be able to answer the questions: "Where did you get your numbers?" and "What thinking led you to this estimate?"

Your document should be clear and concise, with just enough information to evaluate and improve your budget throughout the year.

Step 5: Check Your Figures—Then Check Them Again

You need to check your numbers carefully—and have someone else check them, too. It's difficult to catch your own errors. Have a colleague read your figures aloud while you verify them.

Step 6: Deliver Your Budget

Your manager is likely to want to go over the budget carefully before it goes to Accounting and Finance. This is the first step in the review process. Look at this as your trial run. It's a good opportunity to review your numbers and your assumptions.

Next comes your review by Accounting or Finance, which may or may not want to see your budgetary assumptions. Some financial departments will not want to see all of your notes but will want certain very specific items. Ask them for their guidelines and samples of the terminology they want you to use. You'll want to follow their lead in presenting information appropriately.

When all is said and done, your numbers will be put into the computerized accounting system, and you'll know exactly what funds you have available for the next fiscal year.

Recordkeeping

Good records will help you administer your company's HR policies with great efficiency, eliminating guesswork. Efficient recordkeeping will help prove your compliance with government recordkeeping and reporting requirements. Also, your records provide documentation to defend your decisions on such matters as hiring, discipline, and compensation.

What Records to Keep

HR records should track the "who, what, where, when, and why" of employees. Your main employee file should have a separate record for each employee, and should include the following employee information:

- Employment application
- Job title
- Job description
- Classification (exempt or nonexempt from overtime)
- Offer letter
- Hire date
- Pre-employment tests
- Salary history
- Drug test results
- Background check information, including reference checks
- Employment contracts, if applicable
- Authorization for release of information
- Benefit election forms
- Signature acknowledging review of company policies and receipt of employee handbook
- Résumé
- Skills inventory
- Performance evaluations
- Transfer documents
- Discipline
- Grievances
- Performance goals
- Scheduled training and completed training records
- Copies of the "Help Wanted" ads, Internet postings, and other tools used in the recruiting effort, if the employee is in a federally protected group or you have a government contract (United States of America/Europe)
- Termination documents

- COBRA election forms (USA)
- An exit interview report, if the employee has left the company
- Severance agreements and releases

Some HR records must be kept separately from the main employee file.

These are records containing confidential or sensitive information and include the following:

- Medical records or other records containing medical information
- EEOC documents (such as documents related to a complaint of discrimination) (USA)
- Self-identification forms for EEOC (USA)

Also, some records should be kept in completely separate files in case the organization is audited. These would include:

- Safety records
- I-9 forms (USA)

Important Note: Recordkeeping requirements are addressed in federal and, oftentimes, state laws in the United States of America. Consult legal resources to determine if you are in compliance with state and federal recordkeeping requirements.

For recording employee information, you should develop forms that provide for consistency. This will allow you to demonstrate that employees are treated fairly. An electronic directory of forms is provided with this manual. Please see indexes at the end of this book for a sample of printed legal copies of forms needed by the HR practitioner.

Recruiting

At one time, placing an ad in the "help wanted" section of the newspaper was the primary way to recruit. Now recruitment can (and must) reach a more diverse segment of the population—a group that is accustomed to receiving its information through the Internet, e-mail, television, radio, and direct mail. Employers are also exploring online connections and networking as businesses and employees increasingly connect through internet websites to expand their contacts. Many highly qualified candidates use these sites (e.g., Facebook and LinkedIn®) for job searching and professional networking. Employers can tap into this market of potential candidates when looking to fill positions. As a result, HR must design varied and creative recruiting techniques to locate the best employees.

Why has attracting the right employees become more important than ever? Because bringing in the wrong people can become an expensive mistake, given the high cost of training new workers and the increasing likelihood of being sued for discrimination or wrongful discharge in the event that they are fired.

In a competitive market, the best employees are not going to fall into your lap. If you want to attract top talent, you'd better get busy marketing your organization.

Prospective and new employees have to be treated like customers.

Although some industries are enjoying a surfeit of qualified candidates, others, particularly service organizations, are finding it harder to find qualified, top-notch job candidates. Gone are the days of leaving candidates hanging for weeks wondering whether an offer will be made or not.

Your entire recruiting process should reflect the core values of the organization and make people feel special. The process must be convenient, fast, and accurate. Before you start, make sure you know exactly what type of person is required.

Before You Recruit

You can't hire the best person for the job if you don't know all the specifics about the job opening. Exactly what are the job's description and duties? What kind of experience and education is required? The answer to these questions will help you identify the requirements you will list in advertisements and other recruiting efforts.

To start, meet with the manager who has put in the job requisition or with a small group of people who are very knowledgeable about the job. Ask about the job's duties in detail. Ask what knowledge, skills, and abilities in ideal candidate would need to excel at the job. Once you are comfortable that you know the facts, use the information you have gathered.

- List the duties or work to be performed. Of course, the selection of duties should be fine-tuned to the future needs of the organization. However, unless these future needs are clearly defined and specific, it is best to remain with actual duties being performed.

- Define the level of responsibility related to each task or duty. Make sure to include decisions made by the person in the course of the work, supervision responsibilities, and communication responsibilities.

- Rate the importance of the tasks and the frequency (a percentage of the day, week, or month is easy to work with) each is performed. Look at the top 10 to 15 most important, along with any very frequent tasks not included.

- List the knowledge, skills, and abilities it takes to perform each task well. Count the number of times any knowledge, skill, or ability is used. Rank-order them by how often they occur. Also include knowledge, skills, and abilities that are associated with the top five most important tasks.

- Eliminate any skills, abilities, or knowledge that can be acquired in 1 to 6 weeks. Also eliminate skills and knowledge that are specific to your organization (such as specific work practices). You don't want to require anything that would form a barrier to your considering a top- notch candidate from outside your organization.

- Determine the education and experience needed. Look at each of your top knowledge, skills, and abilities in turn. Consider the desired and result, level of responsibility, and importance of performing correctly when applying the knowledge or skill and when using a given ability. To help you with this analysis, it is good to refer back to your original list of tasks. Decide the level of training and education needed to gain this knowledge, skill, or ability. The highest level of training or education necessary to perform acceptably is the educational minimum requirement.

- Double-check your decisions by looking again at these same skills and knowledge in conjunction with the job's most important tasks, level of responsibility, and importance of performing correctly. But this time, consider two other factors:

—The type of work a person must do in order to learn what is needed for the job

—The amount of time on the job it would take to perform the associated tasks at an acceptable level.

If your recruitment efforts are successful, you can screen for greater experience and education. Doing this type of analysis is time consuming, but well worth it. It just may be the most important step in the hiring process, because knowing what is needed is the best way to ensure the organization gets staffed appropriately.

Marketing Your Organization

How does HR use marketing? Not that much different from how you would market any product. Customer research, if done properly, will tell you about the needs of your prospects. Is it benefits, stability, working at a company that attracts the right people? The research should include what makes people fail or leave, so you can address any issues within the organization.

Marketing also means infusing the entire hiring process with the company brand and values.

- **Get the paperwork over with quickly;** if possible, do it on the same day of the interviewee's initial interview.

- **Be clear about company expectations** about attendance, grooming, behavior, compensation, and promotion—before the candidate is made an offer.

- **If you can, make an offer the same day the person is interviewed** (or completes the interviewing process), or if that's not possible, then let the candidate know when to expect to hear.

- **Avoid raising false expectations;** if it is clear the person won't get the job, be honest about why. Even disappointed candidates will appreciate being treated with that level of respect.

And finally, use your research and marketing skills to be selective and specific about whom you hire. If you do a good job of positioning who it is you are looking for and what is expected, candidates will help you by self- selecting to a certain extent.

Recruitment Sources

There are numerous ways to recruit applicants for your company. Even if you are working with a limited budget, you can still get good results from some of these methods.

Applications on File

The first place to look for potential hires is your application file. These job candidates have already sought employment with your company. This file costs you nothing to review. You can build up an archive of applications by electronically scanning hard-copy applications and turning them into computer files. With an electronic archive, you can search for an applicant on the basis of any information field contained in the documents.

Note: There is a potential risk in maintaining an application file indefinitely—such a file could be requested in a lawsuit (in the USA or Europe) as documentation of discrimination or other unlawful hiring process. The benefits of maintaining an applicant file should be weighed against this risk. An alternative might be a policy of maintaining an applicant file for a limited time span and then discarding the file.

Promotion from Within

Your company can reap rewards by promoting employees from within to senior positions as they become available. If your employees see that your company has a policy of upward mobility, it will have a positive effect on morale. And that, in turn, increases productivity and reduces turnover. Promotion from within—and interdepartmental transfers—yields more experienced employees who are already familiar with the company culture.

Job Postings

Posting in-house job openings can be an excellent means of encouraging current employees to take advantage of promotional opportunities. Post all new jobs in a conspicuous place, such as the company bulletin board. The postings should be available to all employees, including those who work in satellite offices or telecommute, via the company intranet or e-mails. You'll also need to decide how long you want to post the job before opening it up to external candidates.

Employee Referrals

A common recruitment source is word-of-mouth referral from employees and supervisors. Some companies pay an incentive bonus to employees who refer individuals who are ultimately hired and stay a predetermined time. One concern to be aware of is that referrals may, depending on your organization, limit the diversity of candidates for a position.

Employment Advertisements

While the classified ads in most newspapers are still widely read, employment ads now are generally placed online. There are hundreds of sources for you to advertise job leads online, as well as to review résumés posted by jobseekers. Other sources include trade publications, alumni magazines, and professional journals.

Online social networks allow employers another way to interact with potential job candidates and recruit applicants. Some networks provide ways for employers to post open employment positions. Social networks can be an effective tool for finding "passive jobseekers" who may be qualified and interested in the position you have open, but who are not actively looking for a new job.

Blind ads are sometimes used because employers don't want their employees or competitors to know they are seeking job applicants, or they don't want applicants phoning or walking in.

No matter what media you use to post your help wanted ad, keep copies of all your ads and record the number of responses and hires. This can help in determining the effectiveness of specific ads or particular venues.

Phrase your advertisements carefully. Always use gender-neutral job titles. For example, use "Supervisor" instead of "Foreman."

"Wait Staff" instead of "Waitress" or "Waiter." In some job categories, requiring a high school or college degree may be discriminatory. Instead, say "degree or equivalent experience."

Employment Agencies and Headhunters

Employment agencies and headhunters can be a useful source of job candidates. Using an agency saves time, and it can increase your access to qualified applicants. However, this ease of use needs to be balanced with the fee charged.

Recall from Layoff

If you have had a recent downsizing, you may have a significant pool of talented former employees to consider recalling for employment.

Sources of Diverse Applicants

To increase the diversity of your applicant pool, you can develop relationships with diverse community groups and professional organizations. Attending career fairs sponsored by organizations such as the Urban League will help you attract minority candidates. Some organizations, such as the AARP, establish partnerships with employers and provide employers' job application links on their websites.

Colleges and Universities

Placement offices at educational institutions are an excellent source for finding entry-level professionals.

State Employment Offices

State Departments of Labor offer placement resources to all jobseekers, and state Departments of Unemployment Compensation operate job referral offices for unemployment recipients. Many qualified candidates become available as a result of layoffs and downsizing. Your state DOL will work with you—and may even supply training—to meet your needs.

Job Fairs

Not so popular in Third World Countries. There are many opportunities for using job fairs in your recruiting. Sponsor your own, join forces with other companies, or attend job fairs held by other organizations such as chambers of commerce and colleges.

Alternative Staffing

You can meet many of your staffing needs with temporary, part-time, or contract workers. You can also lease employees from other firms, or call back retirees from your own company.

Hiring and Interviewing

Getting those résumés in is just the beginning. Once you sort through them and narrow down your list of likely candidates, it's time to start calling people in for interviews.

Choosing Candidates to Interview

Start sorting résumés with the most concrete requirement, usually education. If you have decided that a B.S. degree is necessary, then start out by placing all of the résumés indicating possession of a B.S. degree in one pile (or electronically, in one folder). Then you can analyze these for the other basic requirements.

If you still have too many candidates to interview in the allotted time, then narrow the field to those candidates with the most desirable abilities. (The desirable abilities can be determined by going back to your job analysis, discussed in the previous section.) Look at the top tasks and at the abilities needed. Determine what level of experience and training is needed to perform very well.

Another way of prioritizing résumés is to choose candidates who have experience performing any of the top duties. Consistency is essential.

Always double-check your sorting. It is easy to make a mistake in this process because of the unique nature of résumés. Of course, no consideration of race, sex, or national origin is appropriate. Just be consistent and choose the best-qualified individuals to interview.

Conducting the Interview

A job interview, like all selection devices, must be designed to measure the important knowledge, skills, and abilities you identified in the job analysis you previously performed. A structured interview process designed to assess past behaviors and accomplishments is best. Here are some guidelines from experienced interviewers:

- Ask candidates to indicate how and in what way they perform duties that require the skills you want to assess.

- Ask all candidates the same questions; 5 to 15 questions is a good benchmark to follow.

- Follow each of these skills-based questions with questions designed to find out the person's level of knowledge and ability.

- Dwell on a few questions in depth. You will understand the capabilities of a candidate better by finding out a lot about their experience in relation to one or two projects they worked on that are closely associated with the work you will assign.

Here is an example of what you might need to know when hiring a maintenance director:

- A general overview of the person's experience supervising trades people

- The trades involved

- What the person was building or maintaining

- A description of responsibilities

- Two or more problems the person faced related to skilled trades work and the solutions he or she employed

By asking follow-up questions, you should gain a good understanding of the person's knowledge of skilled trades work, supervision of that work, and ability to solve problems.

It is a good idea to have another person help you interview so that perceptions of answers can able shared and analyzed. It is also a good idea to use a rating sheet on which you have written the knowledge and abilities you are measuring. Rating candidates will help you make comparisons.

Be sure to take good notes so that you can verify some of this information with the candidate's supervisor when you make your reference check. The notes will also help you compare candidates.

Qualities of the Ideal Interviewer

Do you have the knowledge, skills and abilities needed to be an effective interview? Here's a list of traits to benchmark against:

- **Communication skills.** Interviewees will be more likely to open up to someone who shares their job vocabulary and shows that he or she is able to discuss job content intelligently.

- **Knowledge of jobs in the industry.** The interviewer must be acquainted with industry jobs in order to compare and contrast the job under study with positions in the firm and in the industry as a whole.

- **Judgment and analytical ability.** The interviewer must not only be able to comprehend what the employee is saying, but also be able to probe for additional facts and to weed out subjective or extraneous information.

- **Objectivity.** There is no room in job analysis interviewing for preconceived ideas, personal biases, or extreme opinions.

- **Understanding of human behavior.** The success of the interview depends heavily on the interviewer's ability to motivate the potential employee to respond openly and honestly. The interviewer must develop rapport and encourage cooperation while minimizing suspicion, hostility, and embarrassment.

- Favorable personality traits for interviewers include sincerity, integrity, and the ability to get along with all types of people.

Checking References

You'll want to narrow your list to the most qualified candidates before verifying such basic requirements as years of experience and education. You can require written documentation, such as college or high school transcript, to verify education.

However, once the list is narrowed, you should always do a reference check. You want to make sure that you hire the best person, and also because you are liable for any problems that may arise later. For example, if you hire an employee who becomes violent, and who was violent previously with another employer, you are liable for placing that person in the work environment. However, if you have done a thorough reference check, then the courts have generally found that you are not liable for a bad- hiring decision.

Make notes regarding the basic questions you asked and the answers you received, making sure to indicate whom you spoke to. Along with the questions you will ask concerning qualifications, you should ask how the person was to work with and if there were any problems. Make sure to inquire regarding the candidate's ability to follow instructions and receive constructive criticism.

When checking references, talk to the applicant's supervisor or someone who actually reviewed and saw the quality of the work performed by the person. A second choice is an administrator or a person who has seen the results of the work performed.

Most of the questions you need to ask will be easily generated from the minimum requirements you have previously established. For instance, if you have determined that supervisory experience is important, you would likely ask the following questions:

- Has Isha been a supervisor with your company? For how long?
- How many people was she responsible
- Did she evaluate them?

- Was she able to organize, plan, and direct the work of this group well? If the answer to this question is yes, then ask:

- What work process or problems did she improve or change? At this point, you need to ask follow-up questions until you understand exactly how well this person was able to direct the work of others.

- Do you believe the people under this person did their best? If the answer to this question is yes, then ask:

—What did you observe that draws you to this conclusion?

—Would you hire this person again?

—How do you see this person in the _____ job?

—Would you hire this person to fill a _____ position?

At this point, you need to ask as many follow-up questions as necessary to understand the "why's" behind the answers.

Make sure to keep the results of your reference checks confidential. They should not be in the employee's personnel file, where he or she could see them. If you divulge what a reference said to you, you might be unable to get candid information in the future.

Note: Unfortunately, many employers fearing slander claims have instituted policies prohibiting performance or character references. These employers will only verify dates of employment and, sometimes, compensation rates. In these cases, you may be forced to go to previous employers who employed the applicant prior to their current job or to rely on personal references.

Picking the Best Candidate

It is always nice to have several top candidates to choose from. In this case, pick the person whose abilities are most closely associated with the problems or challenges of the organization; whose skills complement or balance the abilities in the work group; or who seems to have formed working relationships in the past, that are best for the work group at hand. (Likability is dangerous. Always tie your decision back to the important tasks of the position.) If several people have interviewed the candidates, gather these people together to discuss the matter.

Resources

See Appendices on:
- Application Forms Checklist
- Interview Evaluation Form
- Employment Agreement Form
- Application Checklist
- Orientation Checklist

Leadership and Team Building

As a Single HR practitioner, you have a dual role:
- You have to demonstrate your leadership qualities everyday in how you manage yourself and your duties.
- You have to help develop the leadership qualities of the people in your organization.

Your Leadership Role

In many organizations, HR professionals are not seen as leaders. Too often, they are perceived as reactive rather than proactive. For the HR people to truly be seen as leaders, they need to act like leaders. Some of the key components of leadership needed in today's organizations include the ability to:
- Anticipate the changing needs of the organization and act quickly and decisively.
- Continually challenge how you currently do things and seek better solutions.
- Be an agent of change by suggesting innovative, flexible solutions to line management problems.
- Communicate and reinforce the need for continuous learning and constant improvement.

- Embrace technology and use it to provide managers and employees with faster, better-quality service.

HR people who work in pairs or groups may have the luxury of letting others take a leading role in the department. As a department of one, you can't do that. The leadership role is yours alone. You can ignore it and stay in your office, doing paperwork and making phone calls. The fact that you are reading this manual, however, shows that you accept—and even welcome—the position you are in. It takes courage to be the only HR person in an organization, and that's one quality that true leaders all share.

Developing Effective Leaders

One of your key responsibilities is staff development, and in no area is that more important than in developing leaders. Among your organization's employees are people whose innate leadership qualities may be untapped and whose talents and skills are underutilized. Your job is to help managers look for and recognize these next-generation leaders when they find them.

Your organization needs strong leadership if it is to gain and maintain a competitive advantage. Here are some strategies getting leadership development high on the radar screen of your company's management team.

- **Challenge your managers to think about the stars on their team.** Who would they turn to keep things going if they were out? How are they preparing these people to take on a future leadership role?

- **Make sure that future leaders are given opportunities to stretch their skills** and show what they can do.

- **Encourage managers to cross-train individuals** within their department and even among departments. Job swapping allows future leaders to see a wider scope of what the organization needs and what it does. Cross-training may also allow a previously unrecognized individual to show new abilities and competencies.

- **Identify the "uncrowned" leaders in your organization.** Every group has them—the people whom others turn to with problems and questions. These people often don't have the management title, but they practice leadership every day.

Developing leaders can be a risk business. You may find that the person you thought was ideal is just not able to coach others effectively, no matter how hard you work with her, or that someone who has loads of natural leadership ability has no ambition to be in a management role. In this aspect of your job, even when your plans may not work out, you can't lose, because every employee you work with will benefit in some way.

Building a Winning Team

If there's one corporate environment, it's change. Companies have to change—and change quickly—in response to economic and market conditions, customer desires, technological advances, and competitive pressures. One person cannot drive that type of corporate change, and even a small team can't do it. What is needed is to involve every employee at every level in helping the organization succeed. In other words, what is needed is teamwork.

Initiatives to involve employees in the quality of their work have been a regular feature of HR management for years. Employee involvement, participative management, quality circles, and self-managed teams are some of the better-known applications of the principle that people are more motivated to perform when they see and feel that they have an impact on the whole.

The reason that the team approach has remained popular is that a well- functioning team can play a critical role in how your workplace functions. Productivity and morale will skyrocket when workers feel that they are crucial to the success of your organization. Not every supervisor or manger understands how to build an effective team. That's where you come in.

Although you'll read about training in detail in Chapter Three, team building is so critical to your success as a department of one that I am including it right up front.

Effective Teams = High Morale

Study after study has shown that money isn't the driving force behind job performance. Rather, employees are most strongly affected by:

A sense of achievement: to feel that they are working toward something that matters

- **Recognition:** to know that their efforts are valued and appreciated

- **Participation:** to know that their opinions count and that they have some control over their work and environment

- **Growth:** to feel that what they do fulfills their potential

Morale improves when employees see that their performance and ideas really do count and that their actions affect others.

The qualities that define an effective team are the same qualities that you find in a supportive, motivating culture. So by helping to foster effective teamwork, you are helping to raise morale. How, exactly, does this work? Consider these hallmarks of an effective team member, and you'll see how a person working in that environment feels good about himself and his job:

- **Members have a shared concept/vision of where they want to go.** They look to the future rather than dwelling on the past or focusing only on immediate demands.

- **Agreement about their overall purpose helps team members set priorities and assign tasks that are meaningful.** People feel they're making a specific contribution for a valued result.

- **Thinking in terms of a team helps people enjoy the feeling of belonging to a group.** Knowing that others depend on their work is a good motivator.

- **Team members develop a sense of responsibility to the group** and feel more committed to goals they helped establish themselves.

- **As individual roles develop and change, opportunities for learning expand.** Members of a team get the benefit of learning from one another.

- **In effective teams, members feel free to discuss and argue their points of view safely.** They feel that others really listen and respect their point of view.

- **Because the team sets goals, priorities, and tasks, there is a way of evaluating and recognizing achievement.** This makes work more satisfying.

Getting Managers Onboard

In an ideal world, all managers and supervisors would recognize that team building is one of their top priorities. In the real world, or course, it just doesn't work that way. Not every manager is a proponent of teams, and even those who are may not know how to lead teams effectively. Of course, that's where you come! Your challenge is to lead the manager so he or she can lead the team.

Managers will be effective team leaders if they can let go of the desire to control every function and truly delegate power and authority. The bonus for them is that by establishing a genuine climate of participation in their work groups, they will benefit from improved morale and productivity. Help them to understand that reaping the benefits of a well-functioning team also requires changes on their part.

Managers who are effective team builders are people who:

- Believe it's worth the time and effort
- Are willing to share responsibility
- Agree to let go of "authority" and work with subordinates in a more equal fashion
- Are open to change
- Want to share knowledge and information
- Have and show respect for the people they work with
- Will risk being honest
- Listen well—or are willing to improve their listening skills
- Enjoy working with groups of people, not just one-on-one
- Will follow through on plans and ideas coming from the group

- Are willing to make sure others follow through
- Praise, coach, challenge, and inspire
- Have the support of their managers—and of you

Assessing the Effectiveness of Teams

As you work on building effective teams, don't forget to assess how well your organization's teams are doing. Use this checklist to ensure that your teams are truly on track.

The effective team:

- Is open to ideas
- Maintains a high level of commitment
- Adapts to change
- Possesses sound problem-solving skills
- Feels challenged and creative
- Is tolerant of all ideas
- Encourages full participation by all members
- Keeps focused on its goals
- Becomes valued by senior management
- Trusts its leaders, facilitators, and administrators
- Produces quality decisions
- Achieves its goals
- Is rewarded by its company or department

Succession Planning

HR experts uniformly urge companies—whether large enterprises or small, closely held "Mom and Pop" outfits—to begin creating a succession plan by identifying the company's important human assets. Experts emphasize that such "stars" are not only senior executives, but also middle- level technical people who are almost irreplaceable because of their unique skills, institutional memory, or industry contacts.

Companies that push succession planning down the organizational ladder are better positioned to maintain their stride should key players suddenly depart, for whatever reason. Succession planning should be especially essential for companies where there has been high turnover or high growth.

Succession planning can be categorized into four stages:

1. The first stage is a basic replacement plan—a risk-management device that enables a business to replace a fallen leader, whether from a plane crash, heart attack, or sudden leave-taking. Companies new to succession planning should start at this first stage. Even an organizational chart that shows two to three people to fill each position is useful.

2. The second stage of succession planning takes the logic of the initial stage and pushes it downward in the organization to identify replacements for senior-level managers at middle levels of the organizational chart.

3. At the third stage, companies dig beneath the corporate hierarchy to assess the competencies they need to flourish. At this level, you want to start grooming people from within. The goal here is to develop a talent pool from which to draw the needed competencies—for example, up- and-coming craftsmen, innovative product and market managers, or department managers or supervisors who deliver consistently supervisor results from a tightly knit team of workers.

4. Businesses as the fourth stage of succession planning peer outside the company's walls to see who's available in the industry or local marketplace. For example, a company that outsources a portion of its manufacturing may keep its eye on the line manager of that outsourced function as a potential candidate to replace the internal head of manufacturing if necessary.

Another way of ensuring that your organization has the resources on tap to fill critical vacancies is to conduct career development assessments for key employees. Beyond identifying the high-potential leaders of tomorrow, follow through with individually tailored development programs that include training, job rotation, special project assignments, and mentoring by older senior executives.

Employees with leadership potential usually know who they are. Nonetheless, make sure that those special workers who are being groomed for weightier responsibilities know that the company is looking at them for a future leadership position. Letting your internal stars know that they will play a significant role in the company's future may keep them happy and safe behind your walls.

Performance Management

Finding and hiring the best employees is just the beginning. Once those employees come on board, you need a system to help them grow and develop on the job. You need to be able to identify and reward your top performers, both monetarily and with plum assignments that will enhance their skills. And you need to identify sub-part performers and develop plans to either improve their performance or weed them out. In other words, you need a performance management system.

The performance appraisal—also called "performance review" and "performance evaluation"—is the working tool of your performance management system. The appraisal…

- Allows an organization to measure, document, and improve job performance
- Identifies employees who should be promoted or demoted
- Gives formal recognition to outstanding performers
- Provides standards for determining salary increases
- Protects employers from false claims of wrongful discharge and discrimination

That last point is not one to overlook in today's litigious environment.

Decisions regarding promotions, raises, and other rewards are usually dependent on the results of performance appraisals. Unless those decisions are based on objective, job-related, unbiased criteria, they may be subject to claims of discrimination claims.

Companies today are taking many different approaches to formal employee-evaluation systems. Some organizations rely on a brief form of two or three paragraphs, while others use elaborate rating schedules and multipage documents to evaluate their workers. How elaborate a system your organization uses depends on your needs. You may need to use different forms for different categories of employees. However, all appraisal forms should embody these two elements:

1. They should cover all relevant performance criteria.

2. They should be understandable to both the evaluator and the employee.

Rating scales are relatively easy to develop and can be adapted to many kinds of jobs. Various qualities, such as the ability to communicate and dependability, are rated on the basis of a numerical scale. For instance, a score of "5" might mean the employee is outstanding in a category, and a "1" would mean below average.

Accurate, detailed job descriptions are the building blocks of your appraisal system. Use the job analysis techniques described earlier to make sure that all of your job descriptions describe clearly the competencies needed to do the job and the duties the position entails.

Most organizations evaluate employees periodically, usually annually on the 1-year anniversary of each employee's hire date. Some firms review all employees at the same time each year. In either case, when employees are having serious problems with their performance, they should receive performance reviews more frequently.

In almost all cases, the supervisor or manager will be delivering the appraisal to the employee. In some cases where job performance is sub-par, you may choose to sit in on the appraisal with the supervisor. Making sure that your organization's managers and supervisors are thoroughly trained in the specifics of the performance management system and in how to deliver an appraisal is one of your key responsibilities.

Preparing for the Meeting

Before the performance appraisal meeting, the evaluator should gather any records or notes pertaining to the employee's job performance and goals. The employee should be notified of the appraisal meeting at least a week in advance. At this time, the employee should be reminded to complete his or her self-appraisal, if applicable, and to compile any notes he or she wants to bring to the meeting.

The supervisor must then analyze and rate the employee's performance and fill in the appraisal form. You'll need to train supervisors to complete a performance appraisal form in a consistent and standardize manner, based on the work performance over the entire period being evaluated.

Performance should be measured against clearly defined standards and goals set during the previous review and listed in the job description.

Here are some guidelines to provide to those who are responsible for filling in evaluation forms for their employees:

- Use specific, measurable examples to describe job performance and behavior. For example, "Saidu met six of eight sales goals during the past year," as opposed to "Saidu had a good sales record."

- Differentiate job performance from a quality judgment of the person's behavior. For example, "Alinda is consistently 15 minutes late for work daily," not "Alinda is lazy."

- List specific achievements. For example, "Perfect record of reconciling cash terminal during shift."

- Give specific examples of both positives and negatives. Avoid abstract or general comments.

- Avoid the "halo effect" in which one outstanding quality of the worker, positive or negative, is the determining factor in the review.

- Don't permit personal preferences or feelings to influence the appraisal.

- Don't be reluctant to rate an employee unfavorably, if warranted.

- Don't play it safe by rating all employees in the average range.

- List specific ways for the employee to improve. For example, "Increase case contacts by 20 percent."

Conducting the Appraisal

Performance appraisal meetings should always be held in private, and evaluators should do their best to minimize interruptions. By giving the meeting their full attention, evaluators clearly state that they value the performance appraisal process.

During the appraisal, the evaluator should emphasize the development and growth of the employee. Discuss what the employee is doing right before discussing what the employee needs to improve. It's also important to discuss the employee's performance as it relates to the department and the company as a whole. Let the employee know where he or she stands in the big picture.

Encourage questions and suggestions for improvement from the employee. Evaluators will get more buy-in from employees if they actively encourage their participation.

Evaluators should never compare one employee to another. That only causes resentment. Instead, encourage the employee to build and improve on his or her previous performance.

Setting Performance Goals

Throughout the meeting, the supervisor should focus attention on setting those goals that will improve areas of employee performance that are below acceptable levels, as well as goals that help high-achieving employees reach the next level. Though the supervisor will bring a list of prepared goals to the meeting, the employee should be allowed to make a case for changing those goals during the meeting. The employee should understand those areas where job performance can improve, and be ready to take steps to close the gaps in performance.

Performance goals should meet specific criteria. They should be job- related, measurable, observable, attainable, prioritized, written, and agreed on by the employee and the supervisor. Each goal should have a structured action plan to achieve it, and involve the supervisor in regular follow-up meetings to assess progress.

The performance appraisal meeting should not be the only time of the year that employees receive feedback. Ongoing evaluation identifies problems and redirects employees at an early stage and helps avoid blindsiding employees with criticism when their formal appraisal meetings are held. As important as the appraisal meeting is, it should, ultimately, contain no surprises for the employee. If it does, the supervisor has not done an effective job of day-to-day performance management.

Performance and Pay

Research indicates that compensation is just one motivational factor for employees. Other factors, such as job security, employment of work, and friendships with co-workers, also affect employee motivation. More important, the research found that compensation could be a negative motivational factor if employees feel that they are not being compensated fairly. Your challenge is to make sure that you performance management system and your pay structures work in tandem to fairly compensate every employee, from the newest hire to the CEO.

Many organizations are moving toward formal structures that integrate detailed job descriptions and job analyses into a system of graded wage and salary ranges. A system of this kind imposes discipline on supervisors and managers and makes it easier for management to keep payroll growth in check. A formal system, set down in writing with rules that apply to all employees, also makes it easier to communicate the company's pay policies and apply them without bias.

If you have written your job descriptions and have assigned jobs to appropriate grades, you are ready to determine the minimum and maximum rates of pay that should be assigned to each grade. Remember to factor in the cost of living for your organization's geographic locations. There are numerous methods for establishing rate ranges:

- **Adopt ranges used by another branch of your own company.**

- **Adapt or revise the system of ranges you have already established.** However, this may present problems if employees have salaries outside the new range for their jobs.

- **Use rate ranges devised by others in your industry or region.** Many surveys are available for this purpose, including the *Suba-Belleh & Associates* (in Monrovia) and **BLR** (in the United States of America) state-specific wage and salary survey. There are other organizations also capable of setting up this framework for any company.

- **Use a consultant who has experience with setting pay ranges.**

A typical salary range structure has a 50-percent spread from minimum to maximum and a 10-percent difference in grade minimums. Often, the rate ranges are further broken down into thirds to create ranges within ranges. This facilitates a common practice of granting proportionally higher raises to new employees whose pay rates are at the lower end of their grade. A properly structured system will accommodate every job in your organization.

To make a structured system work, managers and supervisors must exercise self-discipline and be willing to hold themselves accountable for pay actions. HR will usually be asked to authorize each pay action to ensure consistency and adherence to the rules.

Many organizations have customized their human resources information system (HRIS) to perform this analysis, ensuring that employees receive raises within their grades, that the raises reflect employees' performance appraisal ratings and that percentage increases are tempered by length of service and current salary level within the pay grade.

Annual Salary Increases

The aggregate salary increase for an organization is usually budgeted by top management each year, using the total amount of payroll and applying a percentage of the total as the overall pay increase amount. This percentage should be based on factors, such as:

- Company profitability
- Cost of living
- Turnover areas
- Comparison rates with market averages

Some organizations have moved away from automatic pay increases, instead basing increases on individual or company performance. Individual salary increases should always be based on performance, as evidenced by regular, formal appraisals. Working with a graded system will make it easier to say within budget targets, since the structure depends on the application of stringent rules.

A popular approach uses two factors in determining the amount of a raise:

1. The individual's performance on the job

2. The individual's position within the range established for the job's grade

If an aggregate pay budget increase is 4 percent, individuals closer to the minimum salary for their grade would be permitted higher percentage increases than those near the top of the grade. However, top performers would quality for higher pay raises, but only within the limits established for their position in the grade.

Periodic adjustments in the rate ranges themselves—and promotions to higher grades—would ensure continued pay growth for high performers who have reached the top of their grade.

Managing Executive Pay

The majority of executives receive pay that consists of base or regular pay, short-term pay (bonuses), long-term stock plans, and/or additional benefits or perquisites. Executive compensation is very complex.

The base pay of executives is just like that of other employees. It should be structured within a salary grade and be subject to market conditions.

Executive salaries are often published in business magazines and websites, especially with today's scrutiny of executive pay.

Incentive pay must clearly be tied to the executive's performance goals and rating, as well as to the company's goals and performance. Also, incentive pay should be administered closely enough to the achievement to motivate the executive to continue high performance.

A long-term compensation plan can consist of stocks in the company, or stock options that give the individual the right to buy stock at some future date, usually at a lower price than market value.

Other forms of executive pay are extra medical or life insurance, or extra perquisites.

Managing Team Performance

In a team-based environment, most employees should share in pay program awards. At the lower levels, rewards should be tied to team performance. At the upper levels, rewards should be tied to both internal and external customer satisfaction. Performance goals will then reflect increasingly complex customer service objectives. In this environment, executives' variable pay programs put greater emphasis on quality improvement and customer service. Top managers are expected to look at the broader issues of market satisfaction, market expansion, and market penetration. Variable pay for executives should emphasize both performance on immediate goals and continued success of the organization.

To make the transition to rewarding process improvements, rather than functional excellence, salary ranges need to be wide enough to incorporate team members. If grades are too narrow, employees are always looking for promotions to get to the next grade, so their focus is on individual efforts rather than on team results. It is also important to minimize the distinctive specialization within the team, whenever possible. Therefore, use the lower end of the salary range to recognize the development of individual skills or primary skills and upward movement through the range to recognize learned crossover skills.

Determine compensation levels by the development of team competencies that are based on both group and individual behaviors. When the team is effective, then all members' pay increases. Of course, in this environment, performance appraisal, especially as it relates to internal and external customer service skills, is crucial.

Team incentive plans succeed best when you follow the following guidelines:

- Incentives are broad and inclusive.
- Time between performance and payout is short.
- There is a clear message that everyone needs to participate in the continuous improvement process.
- Most employees share in incentives.

Resources—See Appendices

- Employee Performance Appraisal Form
- Promotion Policy

Identifying and Solving Problems

To be successful in HR, you need to be fearless. When others shy away from upsetting the status quo, you need to show them that finding problem areas is a good thing. After all, unearthing a problem is the first step in fixing it—and that's how companies grow and prosper.

As I am sure you've found out, however, lots of people think that once the problem is uncovered (and responsibility—or blame—assigned), the job is done. Lucky for them, you can help them avoid making that mistake. After all, the fact that you chose HR as your profession shows that you are solution-oriented!

From Problem to Solution

Whether large or small, we all face problems to some degree, but your focus and approach to dealing with them can make a big difference in your ability to solve them quickly and effectively. The key is developing action- oriented solutions. The first step is to understand the difference between problems and challenges.

Problems vs. Challenges

Problems are obstacles that steal valuable time, energy, and creativity. Because problems are unplanned, they are stressful. Challenges are also obstacles and stressors, but there's a difference. We usually respond to challenges with a sense of control and a belief that we have the ability to overcome or circumvent them. People often face challenges with a positive attitude and positive energy. That's not true with problems.

As you can see, the problem with problems is the high level of negativity.

Why not simply recognize your negative responses and accept that obstacles and changes are a fact of life? By doing this, you are on the way to turning problems into challenges and adopting a more positive attitude.

Accept challenges. Don't ignore them: They won't go away. Most likely, they will just become even more challenging! Instead, when faced with a challenge, try this approach:

- Define the challenge.
- Ask yourself: How anyone solved this challenge or one similar? What can I learn from them?
- Ask yourself: How can I grow, and what can I gain from this challenge.
- Ask yourself: What are my options? Is there something I can give up to solve this challenge?
- Ask yourself: Who can I call on for help?
- Ask yourself: Is there any way I can make solving this challenge fun or enjoyable?
- Take action!

Solving Morale Problems

One of the most frequent challenges facing HR is what one expert defines as "the creeping malaise of bad attitude." In today's stressful economic environment in the world, poor attitudes can thrive. Have increasing productivity, good morale, and teamwork turned to resentment, declining performance, and a generally negative attitude? Are you seeing friction among co-workers and refusals to work together? If so, you've got a morale problem.

The specific causes of poor morale are usually unique to the environment, but they can frequently be traced to a few basic issues: poor leadership, poor employee fit, and poor communication. Let's look at each of these areas, the problems that may arise, and how you can start solving them.

Leadership Problems

Poor leadership at any level within the organization makes everyone's job harder. If the leader doesn't consistently demonstrate high standards through actions and words, employees will behave accordingly and develop increasingly bad attitudes.

Good leadership is a win-win situation for all concerned. Consider the real-life situation where employees in one department were constantly bickering among themselves and had developed a "why bother" attitude. HR identified the main problem as a lack of leadership. The company replaced the department supervisor and clearly restated everyone's job descriptions, including behavior and production expectations. Result: the problem, which could have dragged on for years, was solved in a matter of weeks.

A quick way to test whether an attitude problem stems from poor leadership is to ask these questions:

1. Does a supervisor make an effort to resolve behavior or performance problems? Or problems ignored?

2. Do employees get merit increases automatically, regardless of performance?

3. Are there obstacles, such as inadequate communication or limited access to resources or work tools that prevent proper performance? If the answer is "yes" to any of these questions, experts say it's likely that poor leadership is the primary source of the attitude problem.

Employee Fit

Even individuals with impressive credentials may not fit in with the company culture. If a talented employee behaves in a manner inconsistent with the organization's values or ethical standards, co-workers and others can become confused and antagonistic toward the individual.

Sometimes, companies are so intent on winning the talent war that they make a poor hiring decision. For example, a consulting firm was thrilled to attract a talented individual from another firm. The company already had a sizeable department headed by another competent consultant in the same specialty. So the new consultant reported to an office manager rather than the department head, although she used the department staff and resources to help her complete her assignment.

Within 2 weeks of her arrival, the staff began complaining that they couldn't get their own assignments completed because the new consultant insisted that they attend to her demands first. She also insisted that staff follow her instructions rather than the established department procedures. All efforts to resolve the problem failed, so the new consultant was transferred to another office where she could build her own department from scratch. Unfortunately, her unwillingness to be a team player with consultants in other specialties in the new office resulted in her termination.

Many HR pros say that the best way to avoid this type of situation is to be sure that you include behavioral questions in your interviewing process to help assess the individual's fit with your organization's cultural style, values, and business goals. For example, you might ask:

- What would you do if you strongly disagreed with a team member on how a particular project should be handled?

- What is the largest or most difficult obstacle you have encountered in the work environment? What did you do? How did it turn out?

Communication Issues

Failure to effectively communicate up, down, or with peers causes problems. Some symptoms of attitude problems stemming from poor communication include reluctance to talk or excessive verbalization, failure to listen, and failure to ask questions. These patterns signal the possibility of unspoken issues that are bothering an employee or group. The trick is to get the issues to the surface.

One HR pro who is an experienced facilitator says that conducting an idea-or activities-based meeting is a good place to start. Ask attendees to come to the meeting prepared with a list of three examples of how well the department communicates and three communication-related things that can be improved. Small index cards are good for this exercise. The lists can be anonymous and collected at the beginning of the meeting. Read the cards aloud, record examples on a flipchart, and add a checkmark every time an item is repeated. Solicit additional comments and then have the group prioritize the things that can or should be fixed in the short term.

Brainstorm with the group to identify possible action steps to fix the top three or four issues, and ask the group to select which action steps to implement.

This is just one example of how focused group activities can help solve communication and attitude problems. However, proponents emphasize that using an experienced facilitator is critical to the success of such an undertaking.

A final tip: Because effective communication is more than just writing or speaking words, almost everyone can benefit from periodic communication refresher training. The time invested will pay off in improved communication—and better morale.

Conducting Periodic Audits

Periodic HR audits are a straightforward way to ensure effective use of an organization's human resources and to maintain or enhance HR's reputation within the company. In this section, I will give you a broad overview of the various types of HR audits and reasons for employing them.

Types of Audits

The different types of HR-related audits are designed to accomplish a variety of objectives, including:

- Ensuring compliance with federal, state, and local laws
- Helping maintain or improve a competitive advantage in areas such as compensation, benefits, and recruiting
- Establishing and supervising efficient and well-documented files, record maintenance, and technology practices
- Identifying strengths and weaknesses in training, communications, and other employment practices.

The type of audit you want to conduct and how frequently you do it generally depends on your business needs.

Audits should be conducted initially when taking over the HR function for a company, and during mergers, acquisitions, and start-ups. Then they should be conducted periodically as the organization changes, the community changes, or as laws or standards change. Some things, such as employee relations, compensation, staffing, and training, may be looked at annually depending on need.

Benefits and Pitfalls of HR Audits

Periodic audits allow you to:

- Use audits findings and recommendations to help the company function more efficiently and better serve employees and customers.

- Identify and prioritize risks.

- Improve communications and morale with employees.

- Establish better credibility, communications, and perceptions with senior management.

- Standardize policies and procedures.

- Enhance HR's role as an important part of the organization.

On the other hand, HR audits can complicate your life because sometimes management sees audits as a technique HR uses to "stir up trouble." Other pitfalls include management's resistance to change, which translates into a lack of commitment to recommendations. Also, some recommendations might take years to implement successfully or could cost more than the company can afford or is willing to spend. It's important to factor these drawbacks into your decision making.

Approaches to Conducting Audits

Even with constantly improved technology (such as computer-based questionnaires, analysis, and report-writing tools) designed to simplify and expedite the audit process, some audit steps are decidedly low tech in nature.

For example, you may be able to automatically transfer demographic, compensation, and benefit date from your HR and/or payroll systems into a computer program that twill reassemble it and give you a variety of audit analyses and reports, including highlights of high-risk situations.

However, certain data and information may not be readily available in a form you can input into a computer, for instant analysis and recommendations. Examples include organization charts, policies, handbooks, and other typically print-based tools, such as newsletters, job applications, and other forms (including form letters), as well as unique practices of supervisors, managers, and operating units. For these, you will have to use a lower-tech approach to request and analyze relevant information, such as gathering and reviewing hard copies of print-based materials.

Another valuable exercise is conducting interviews with management and employees in order to document their perceptions and concerns about the company, the HR function, employment practices, career goals, training and development, and health and safety.

You also may need to draw on the expertise of your outside advisors to help ensure that your employment practices comply with all relevant rules/laws of your country.

Once you've collected the basic data and information you need, you're ready to analyze the results. You may want to invite assistance from outside experts at this step. Regardless, careful analysis of the data and information you collect will influence the success of your audit approach.

Simple Job Analysis

Job analysis is the systematic analysis of an existing or proposed position or group of positions within an organization. Understanding and being able to perform good job analysis is an essential HR function forming the basis of selection, promotion, training, and so on. It is the best way to establish what exists, what works, and what should be changed.

Getting Ready

Review previous job analyses, if any exist. Read any recruitment information, such as newspaper advertising and brochures, as well as information given to past applicants. Gain a basic understanding of the current and possible reporting and working relationship between this job and other jobs.

In the case of a new job or positions that have not existed in the organization before, make sure you understand the reasons for the position from the person in highest authority over the position.

Always begin by asking a job incumbent or supervisor to list the duties of the position and then to indicate which are the most important by ranking them, beginning with "1" to indicate the most important task. Then ask them to indicate the five or so duties they spend the most time performing.

Some people stop here, which is acceptable. In the hands of a good analyst, this small job analysis can support several personnel decisions.

Data Gathering

The following techniques are those most often used when gathering data for a job analysis:

- **Observation.** Stand and watch one employee work. This is best used for manufacturing jobs and jobs that are easily discernible by merely knowing what a person physically does.

- **Desk audits.** Go to the employee's work location and ask him or her to walk you through the most important and most frequent tasks. This is a good way to analyze clerical and technical positions.

- **Group interviews.** Gather a group of top performers in a room where interruptions will be minimized. Ask them to explain why certain tasks are more important than others and how tasks are performed. This approach is best used for managerial and supervisory positions or in conjunction with a desk audit when you want to make sure you do not miss anything.

- **Questionnaires.** Use this approach when there are several positions and it is not feasible to bring several employees together for an interview. Prepare the questionnaire by conducting one or more desk audits, brainstorming sessions, or interviews.

- **Diaries.** Ask one or more employees to keep a diary of duties, noting the frequency of the tasks performed.

- **Videotaping.** A videotape of the job being performed can be watched several times to perform analysis and can be pulled out later to reevaluate.

- **Review of records.** Review records of work, such as maintenance requests, and make a list of requested repairs. Take representative samples so that seasonal variations in work requests are not misleading. This is a good approach for such jobs as mechanic or electrician. This approach could also be used for computer programming and computer troubleshooting jobs in which employees have records of work requests or work completed.

The data to be gathered are dependent in large part on the purpose of the analysis. Information about training needs requires information about the transaction of the work so that the trainer can determine the critical skills and knowledge that must be improved. Selection decisions require the same information on a broader scale.

Here are examples of information to gather, depending on your desired purpose:

- List of tasks
- List of decisions made
- Indication of results if decisions are not made properly
- Amount of supervision received
- Supervision exercised
- Kind of personnel supervised
- Diversity of functions performed by supervised staff
- Interactions with other staff
- Physical conditions
- Physical requirements
- Software used
- Programming language used

- Computer platform used
- Customer contact
- Interpersonal persuasive skills or sales skills
- Amount of mental or physical stress
- Necessity to work as a team member
- Needed contributions to a work group
- Authority or judgment exercised
- Customer service skills

To collect all the information you need, you'll have to sue more than one data gathering method. It is best to start out gathering the basic information and then to add methods and other data gathering in an effort to gradually put together an entire true picture.

At the very minimum, you should have a list of tasks and duties, information regarding their importance to the overall performance of a satisfactory employee, and an indication of how frequently these duties are performed. You should be able to describe the basic concept of the job; extrapolate working conditions, skills, and knowledge needed to perform each task; and be able to quantify the minimum qualifications needed in a new employee.

Using the Job Analysis

The most important use of job analysis is to produce a basic job description. When pay is closely associated with levels of difficulty, these descriptions will help foster a feeling of organizational fairness related to pay issues. Other important uses of a job analysis include:

- Indicating training needs
- Forming work groups or teams
- Providing information to conduct salary surveys
- Providing a basis for determining a selection plan
- Providing a basis for putting together recruitment
- Describing the physical needs of various positions to determine the validity of discrimination complaints

- As part of an organizational analysis
- As part of strategic planning
- As part of any human relations needs assessment
- As a basis for coordinating safety concerns

Managing Your Benefits and Compensation Program

Benefits packages are used by employers to remain competitive in order to attract and retain qualified workers. Yet benefits packages must be managed and cost-controlled so as to ease their impact on an employer's bottom line. This is a challenging responsibility for a single practitioner, but one that is essential to the future of your organization.

When assessing your benefits package each year, you should reach the benefits offered by other companies in your industry and in your geographic area. Is your package significantly more or less generous? If it is less generous, you may be at a competitive disadvantage when recruiting and retaining employees. If it is considerably more generous than those of your competitors, you may be needlessly taking money away from the bottom line.

Personal and Professional Development

As an HR department of one, you help employees in your organization develop and grow to meet changing needs. That can be so all-consuming that you put your own career development aside. However, that can be one of the biggest mistakes that a one HR practitioner makes. If you are not minding your career, no one will. As time goes on, you'll fall further behind the ideal HR competency model.

Key Competencies

What are the key competencies necessary for you to excel at your job? I touched on some of the basics in Chapter 1. But as you grow with your job, your competency model should grow and evolve as well. Here are five key competencies that an HR professional must develop in order to impact business financial performance:

1. Strategic contribution is a necessary competency, and it includes 4 subcategories: culture management, fast change, involvement in business decision making, and leveraging customer information to create unified and customer-focused organizations.

2. Personal credibility is another key factor. HR professionals must have effective relationships with key people inside and outside the organization. They must deliver results and establish a reliable track record. In order to accomplish this, they have to be credible to both their colleagues and the employees they serve. In addition to personal credibility, excellent written and verbal communication skills are critical to the HR function, since communication is central to the core activities of the position.

3. Effective HR delivery in six major areas—staffing, development, organizational structure, HR measurement, legal compliance, and performance management

4. Business knowledge is the fourth domain. To become key players in the organization, HR professionals must understand their organizations and the industries in which they work. High-performing HR professionals use this knowledge to make strategic contributions.

5. Technology is increasingly used as a delivery vehicle for HR services. HR professionals need to be able to use HR technology and Web-based channels to deliver services to employees.

It's not a coincidence that strategies for developing each of these five competencies can be found in this book. But the book is just a primer. Once you master what's in these pages, you need to take the initiative to keep learning and keep adding to your skill set.

How to Develop Competency

The complexity of your HR role demands ongoing skills development.

There are no specific academic requirements for human resources managers, but most employers prefer that candidates have at least a Bachelor's degree. Professional education is important in this field, particularly for those who are responsible for benefits administration.

Recommended courses include economics, finance, English, psychology, labor relations, and organizational behavior. The programs that are particularly advantageous for HR professionals seeking to broaden their business knowledge are those resulting in a Master's of Business Administration or Master's in Organizational Development. Here are some of the issues to be aware of as you research schools for additional training.

Accreditation

While there are HR programs that advertise that they are licensed by a particular country, this is not the same as being accredited, since the standards set by accrediting bodies are usually more demanding than the requirements for licensure. If you are involved in a distance-learning program, make sure the program is accredited. Also, be aware that traditional education programs offered by an institution of higher learning can be accredited, while their online programs might not have achieved that status.

Make certain that whatever accreditation a school presents, it is widely accepted by employers and colleges. If you receive a Bachelor's degree that isn't recognized by graduate schools, it may limit your continuing education options.

Choose a program with teaching methods that are consistent with your learning style. Is the instruction set to proceed at a student's own pace, or are there specific deadlines to meet regarding projects, reading, and course completion? Are there opportunities to interact with instructors and other students via e-mail, newsgroups, or in real-time events, such as online conferencing?

Maximize Your Resources

The only way to get your job done is by having the right support, tools, and skills. And as time goes on, your need for resources and support may increase. Unfortunately, it is unlikely that you will be able to fulfill your entire resource wish list. To do more or to do your job better, you have to recognize and maximize your available resources and use your budget effectively.

- **People are your most important resource.** They are the reason you are where you are, doing what you love. Maximize this resource by hiring the most qualified and most enthusiastic people available, providing them with the training and equipment they need to do an excellent job, and working closely with their managers to keep them focused. Make sure their efforts are acknowledged and rewarded in their department and throughout the company. Develop and maintain close relationships throughout your company, and your job will be easier.

- **Invest wisely in the best tools your organization can afford.** Outdated technology and inefficient systems may result in costly problems in the long-term. HR is getting increasingly complex, and devastating legal problems can result from ineffective or inefficient information systems. If your resources cannot be stretched as far as needed, look to such solutions as outsourcing or partnering with another company to recognize efficiencies of scale.

- **Make the most of your time.** Time is a finite resource. How you use it can determine your success or failure. There will always be more tasks than hours available to complete them. Learn how to prioritize in order to make the most of the time you have. Identify and eliminate or reduce time-wasters. Organize your schedule so that you make the most of every day.

- **Take advantage of your internal resources: your knowledge and skills.** Honestly assess the strengths you bring to the job and whether your weaknesses lie. Start pursuing the training, education, or relationships you need to turn your weaknesses into strengths.

Plan and Organize for success

To be effective as an HR department of one, you must set and meet organizational, departmental, and personal goals. Plans are the road you take to meet those goals.

1. Long-term plans cover the broad, key tasks and deadlines.

2. Short-term plans include day-to-day activities. When making short-term plans, write down what you will do, by when, and the desired results.

Use your plans as a guide you refer to regularly to track your progress. But remember: A plan is only a path; it's not the goal itself. You often have to modify your plans to reflect new information or a new strategic direction. Don't get so focused on the plan that you lose track of the goal!

Organization is the tool you use to implement your plans. Organize your day, tasks, and work area so that you can implement plans in an orderly fashion. But organization is not the same as nearness or rigidity. Putting too much emphasis on an orderly work area can be a way to avoid taking action.

Are You Your Own Worst Enemy

Even the savviest HR professionals sometimes act in ways that can stall their careers and harm their effectiveness. One Person HR people, with their pressing responsibilities and no one working alongside them to provide a counterpoint, may be particularly susceptible to these career roadblocks. So here's your own reality check. If you recognize yourself in the statements below, take corrective action now before you become your own worst enemy.

- **"I don't have control."** While you may not have direct control over departments or work groups, you do have influence over managers. Use that influence to show them how to solve problems, get buy-in for new initiatives, and make improvements.

- **"I don't have management approval."** Senior management doesn't want to be involved in the details—that's your job. They are looking at the big picture. So as long as you are clear on the company's strategic direction, you can frequently implement programs that support those goals without getting specific sign-off.

- **"I'm too busy."** HR people are always too busy. But you must be creative in dealing with the small stuff so that you have the time to focus on strategic issues.

- **"There's no money in the budget."** You can gain credibility with management and get the money you need by preparing and managing a budget that aligns your department with the company goals.

- **"Everybody's doing it."** Get off the "HR flavor of the month" bandwagon and makes sure any new initiative you recommend is really right for your organization.

CHAPTER FOUR

TRAINING EMPLOYEES FOR ORGANIZATIONAL EXCELLENCE

First the negative side of recruiting for training

Most HR practitioners in third-world countries lack the fervor to train employees who thrive hard and dedicate their services to keep their organizations running. In most circumstances, foreign training is given to friends or very close relatives of the recruiter or an executive or CEO of the company. Such recruits sometimes lack the educational background or are not even employed with the organization. These friends or relatives sometimes abandon the organization when they shall have returned from the training. Or they would either work for the organization to receive large monthly wages for the benefit of the recruiter's family or give a higher position for the trained employee to have more access to the organization's benefits. It could also result in the employee abandoning the organization for a well-paid job with another organization. This is unethical and lack professionalism. Training should be a benefit to qualified workers who are from the organization's payroll and who have or still serving the organization's mission of establishment. Many workers in third-world countries have suffered greatly in obtaining scholarships or training because they're of a different tribe or are not relatives to an executive or CEO of the organization for which they work.

Some third-world supervisors, HR practitioners and CEOs feel unsafe to recruit from within the organization simply because they fear they might be relived of their positions and given to the overqualified employee on his return from training abroad.

Why Unbiased Recruiting for Training is Good for the Organization.

You may be one-person HR department, but you can't act alone if your organization is to thrive. All people in the organization have to understand and comply with the policies, laws, and procedures that apply to them.

Training is more important today than ever before. The existence of a global economy means increased competition, and you need a highly trained workforce to meet those competitive challenges. Thanks to rapid advances in technology, job-related knowledge goes out of date more quickly today than it did 20 years ago. New regulations pertaining to the workplace often require compliance education and training; this is true of organizations in developed countries.

Benefits of Training

Training should not only be focused on people we know are related or friendly to us or our families. Effective training enables your organization to make the most of its investments and not for your friends or family or family friends, because employees:

1. Develop knowledge and skills that make them more productive and effective.

2. Learn to use equipment and technology properly and effectively.

3. Learn to work in ways that avoid accidents, lawsuits, and government fines—such should be applied in third-world nations.

4. Develop communication, teamwork, and other skills that enhance their contributions to the organization.

Training programs help employees learn how to use new equipment, technologies, and procedures; comply with government regulations; and open their minds to new ways of working. Training keeps employees up to date on issues that affect their jobs. They gain knowledge for immediate use and to serve as the basis for more advanced skills. Training also helps them open their minds to new approaches and thinking about their jobs—a critical point when change initiatives require employees to be flexible and adaptable. Also, training, especially training that helps employees advance their skills, is a valuable benefit.

Training may be formal or informal. It may require one session or many months. It may be required for all employees or for only one. It may take place at work, in college, or at off-site seminars.

Whatever the details, training has to be an ongoing part of everyone's job. It helps us all to make the most of our talents, master new skills, and keep ourselves fresh, productive, and ready for whatever comes up.

The Key Role of Supervisors

Supervisors, who are the organization's front line, play a particularly critical role in this process. They must:

- Understand what training is required by law.

- Know what training resources are available to their employees.

- Understand why training is important in employee motivation and development as well as organizational growth and productivity.

- Identify training needs and topics and decide who needs training.

- Be familiar and comfortable with organizational policies and with employment-related laws.

- Adhere carefully to proper and legal practices and ensure that their employees do the same.

- Make sure that each individual receives fair and respectful treatment.

- Recognize that the situations to which the laws apply aren't always clear-cut.

- Understand the legal issues involved in hiring and firing.

- Know what they can and can't ask applicants and employees.

- Recognize when to get HR involved with employee requests for time off for family and health situations.

- Be committed to protect both the employees' and the employer's rights.

Supervisors, as the employers' representatives, must fully understand employees' rights so that they can avoid violations, respond appropriately to complaints and concerns, and resolve issues before they turn into lawsuits (this should be practiced in third-world countries).

If employees do file charges, the efforts to comply with the applicable laws become even more critical. When courts examine discrimination, retaliation, and other employment claims, they look closely not just at employer policies but also at how those policies were communicated and implemented in the workplace. If they exist only on paper, the employer is in a week position.

That's where you come in. Supervisors need ongoing training to develop the knowledge, skills, and confidence to handle HR-related issues on a daily basis.

Nine Steps to Effective Training

As a one HR person, you'll most likely be the key trainer in your organization. But even if you have limited training experience, you can be a highly effective trainer if you keep these guidelines in mind:

1. Be familiar with your organization's training needs. Plan sessions that focus on the questions, problems, and concerns that supervisors and employees raise.

2. Link concepts, laws, and issues to your trainees' job reality. Use actual (but anonymous people on the job examples. Talk about policies, procedures, and examples that will make your trainees and in recognition. If you have time, encourage participants to provide their own examples.

3. Give trainees a chance to participate. Allow time for questions and discussions (or least a chance to identify topics for follow-up). Discussion helps ensure that participants understand the subject. It also makes the sessions more interesting.

4. Review the session outlines, handouts, and quizzes before the session. Copy handouts and quizzes in sufficient quantities before the training session. You want to be able to distribute them quickly and easily without wasting session time.

5. If you are using quizzes to test understanding of the subject matter, position the quizzes as self-tests. Supervisors, in particular, may feel that they're "above" the short quizzes that conclude each session. Position the quizzes as a useful self-review to help them make sure they understand the topic.

6. Emphasize supervisors' legal responsibilities. Let supervisors know that they are personally responsible for complying with employment laws—and potentially liable for failure to do so.

7. Deliver training briskly, professionally, and authoritatively. Make it clear that you believe in what you're saying and care about getting your message across.

8. Learn from your training experience. Evaluate each session after it's completed and consider what went well or what you feel cold be improved. Make notes from your next session.

9. Allow the students to critique the training session. This input will tell you how well they felt the training was presented. The critique is an excellent method of gaining data to make the next session better. The critique should be written and anonymous, unless you want to discuss the critique later with a particular student.

We'll look at each one of these steps in more detail in the following sections.

Training Preparation: Issues to Consider

Employees are promoted to supervisory jobs because they are strong performers. However, they often lack the knowledge and many of the skills that they need to supervise effectively. They may have little or no understanding of critical employment laws and the key role they play in ensuring fair and legal treatment. Even experienced supervisors may be hard-pressed to keep up with their changing responsibilities and the changing laws and policies that affect them.

Ongoing HR training can help supervisors improve the way they do their jobs and represent their employers. For the training to be effective, however, it must be more than a lecture. The training must relate to supervisors' own jobs and organizations and allow them to discuss and reinforce what they've learned.

Training must also fit into an already crowded work schedule. Neither supervisors nor the organization can afford to take hours out of the workday for training. However, by putting in the time to plan and prepare, you can often provide brief, targeted training sessions in as little as 10 to 15 minutes.

Legal Considerations

Employees must receive regular pay when they take part in training during working hours. In general, if you require an employee to attend training, you must pay the employee for that time, as well as for travel time if the training is off-site.

Employees don't have to be paid if they take training outside of working hours, if it's voluntary, if it's not directly related to the employee's present job, and if it doesn't require any productive work during the program.

Topics for Training

How do you decide what topics to train on? Some training, such as safety training or training in sexual harassment prevention may be mandated by the federal and/or state requirements. The following are training topics you should consider for your training program:

Sexual harassment. Employees should receive training to eliminate sexual harassment from the workplace. The United States Supreme Court has ruled that employers may be held liable for sexual harassment if they do not exercise reasonable care to prevent and promptly correct any such behavior—even if they were not aware of the specific actions in question.

This decision highlights the importance of sexual harassment training. Training should not be a one-time event but must be repeated for all new employees and held at least annually for all employees. Some states require sexual harassment training.

Diversity. Many companies also provide diversity training for all employees. Diversity training is an attempt to create a workforce in which employees of both genders and all ages, ethnic groups, races, and religions, as well as those with disability, are able to work together harmoniously. Having a diversity training program can help minimize discrimination problems that can lead to claims under the fair employment laws.

Orientation. New employees will need training in the specifics of their job and of how your company works. Supervisors may need training when you introduce a new performance appraisal system, and almost everyone can benefit from training on such topics as time management.

Skills training. All employees can benefit from skills training. Specific skills training may benefit individuals whose shills are well ahead of or behind the group. Top performers may view training in advanced skills as a reward. And by training top performers, you can make the most of slim training budgets—and of being a one-person department—by having those top performers help spread new knowledge to other workers.

Struggling employees may need extra training to rise to the level of other employees. Training should be an opportunity, not a punishment, for these struggling performers.

Don't overlook training in so-called "soft" skills. Communication, time management, and other personal skills training can help employees improve job performance. Employees may also view personal skills training opportunities as a reward and motivation. And improved personal skills can help employees work more effectively with co-workers, customers, vendors, and management.

The **Occupational Safety and Health Act** requires safety training, including:

Emergency evacuation and procedures. Before implementing an emergency action plan, employers must designate and train a sufficient number of people to assist in the safe and orderly emergency evacuation of employees.

Fire hazards. Employers must make known to employees the fire hazards of the materials and processes to which they are exposed.

Personal protective equipment (PPE). Employers must train every worker who is required to use PPE. Training must cover, at a minimum: what PPE is necessary; when it is necessary, how to wear, use, and adjust the particular PPE; its proper care, maintenance, useful life, and disposal; and its limitations. If an employee who has already been trained does not appear to have a good understanding, the person must be retrained.

Employers must provide training in the use and care of all hearing protectors provided to employees.

Respirators. Employees using respirators in their jobs must be trained in procedures to ensure adequate air quality, quantity, and flow of breathing air for atmosphere-supplying respirators. Training should also cover the respiratory hazards to which workers are potentially exposed during routine and emergency situations, and the proper use, maintenance, and limitations of respirators.

Processes and operations. Each employee presently involved in operating a process, or before operating a newly assigned process, must be trained in the operating procedures, with emphasis on the specific safety and health hazards, emergency operations including shutdown, and safe work practices applicable to the employee's job tasks. Refresher training should be provided at least every 3 years, and more often if necessary.

Rights to know/hazard communication. OSHA's hazard communication standard (HCS) requires employers to provide employees with information and training on hazardous chemicals in their work area. The training must be given at the time of the initial assignment and whenever a new hazard is introduced into the work area. Training must be specific to the kinds hazards present in the workplace and the particular protective equipment, measures, and procedures that are necessary. General training or a general discussion of hazardous chemicals, for example, is not enough. At a minimum, the training must cover the following:

- The location of workplace areas in which hazardous chemicals are present and where the workplace chemical list, material safety data sheets, and the written communications program are kept.

- How the hazard communication program is implemented, how to read and interpret labels and material safety data sheets (MSDSs), and how employees can obtain and use available hazard information.

- How workers can detect the presence of hazardous chemicals (e.g., visual appearance, smell), their physical and health hazards, and protective measures employees can take, including specific protective procedures the employer is providing such as engineering controls, work practices, and personal protective equipment.

Training Resources

In these times of tight budget, money for training can be hard to find. Government programs may subsidize some training, including the following:

- Disadvantaged new employees entering the job market
- Retraining workers with obsolete skills or facing layoffs
- Retraining workers facing layoff
- School-to-work and other youth training programs

You may also be able to work with outside nonprofit groups to provide training for people with physical or mental disabilities and people with little or no reading skills. Unions or trade groups may work with you to set up and help fund apprenticeship programs.

Documenting Training

With all you have to do as a one practitioner, it may seem that documenting training is just one more task on an already endless to-do list. But the few minutes you take to document training sessions are well worth it.

Documenting your training efforts serves several purposes:

- It helps you track your efforts and see who was trained, what they were trained on, and what future training might be needed.

- Because training program participation and presentation must be free of discrimination, documenting your training efforts provides a record that all employees have fair and equal access to training.

- It provides proof to such agencies as OSHA that you are complying with federal and state training requirements.

The basics of documentation show how, why, and to whom training was presented. In addition, by going beyond the basics and documenting individual successes and failures in training, you will be in a position to follow up with additional training where necessary.

Choosing the Right Mode of Training

How can you ensure that the training you offer employees will actually result in better job performance? You can improve the odds that workers will incorporate new skills into everyday job behavior if you do the following:

- Use training technologies that build how-to skills that are highly relevant and immediately applicable on the job.

- Stay away from theoretical or inspirational training approaches. Concrete, hands-on training is best.

- Follow up on training sessions with on-the-job coaching and support from managers.

- Build training around organizational objectives and strategies.

- Involve senior management.

- Make your training sessions entertaining and enlightening.

No one type of training is right for every organization and every topic. In this section, we are going to take a look at some of the most common training techniques that HR practitioners use.

On-the-Job Training

This hands-on, one-to-one type of training is essential for teaching many new skills to both incoming and other employees. Demonstration is often the only effective way to teach employees to use new equipment or to teach the steps in a new process. Combined with the opportunity for questions and answers, this is a powerful and engaging form of training.

On-the-job training also offers the opportunity for veteran employees to work side by side with newer employees to transfer knowledge, skills, and experience.

Classroom Training

Lectures, discussion, videos, PowerPoint® presentations, and other presentations disseminate essential information, teach new skills, and refresh already learned material on a regular basis. The advantage of bringing employees together for training includes the possibility for group discussion and problem-solving as well as the "human touch," which so often enhances learning. There are a number of advantages to training that take place in a classroom with a qualified instructor:

- Face-to-face instruction gives trainees an opportunity to ask questions and engage in group discussions.

- Classroom training has proved to be very effective when the goal is preventing or solving problems.

- Trainees usually listen to and respect an instructor who is an acknowledged expert in his or her field.

Instructor-led training also has its drawbacks, however. Not every trainee in the class has the same training needs or requires the same level of instruction. Different instructors within the same training program may not cover exactly the same information. Trainees who arrive late, ask too many questions, or need assistance waste too much time. And unless students are tested at the beginning and at the end of the program, there is no way to telling whether classroom training has been effective.

Computer-Based Learning

Technology has made new approaches to training possible. E-learning— presenting training materials through the Internet or an internal company network (intranet)—enables employers to train workers right at their desktop computers.

- E-learning poses distinct advantages that classroom-based instruction does not share:

- Employees can digest training materials at their own pace.

- Everyone receives the same content delivered in the same way, so training is more consistent.

- E-learning is less expensive to deliver than traditional classroom training.

- Training can be given by experts who are off-site or who have formulated prewritten lessons.

The main advantage of a variety of high-tech approaches to employee training is flexibility. Employees can train individually whenever it is most convenient for them and their supervisors. Computer-based training is also a boon for the one HR practitioner because the sessions are developed and ready to use, with a minimum of your preparation time.

Several reasonably priced and easily implemented opinions make this form of training extremely attractive. Suba-Belleh & Associates and other expert companies in Liberia and BLR in the United States of America offer a number of training resources to meet the needs of HR practitioners. Search the HR catalog directory of training of employees in your country to find companies that are qualify to offer such training to your employees, including the Ministries of Labor and Education and the institutes of Management for Personnel Services.

Getting the Most from Your Training Sessions

How do you develop a training program that will capture the attention of your audience, teach them what they need to know, and motivate them to excel? Here are some secrets to training success.

Effective Training Techniques

Make it fun. Don't bore your audience with complicated concepts and theory. They want to know how to get better results, not what the latest statistics say. Get the information across in plain language, and keep it lively by using a variety of media—audiovisual, written material, and interactive training (including role-laying). Humor can be very effective in keeping interest and enthusiasm up. And don't underestimate the importance of attractive-looking materials.

Make it interactive. Instead of sitting and listening to a speaker, have participants tell stories, play games, and role-play different scenarios all related to the material being taught.

Make it hands-on. Experiential training means that participants learn by actually practicing the skills being taught and by relating their own experiences on the job to the material being taught. Experiential training respects the knowledge and experience of the participants and builds on it to enhance practical learning that can be immediately transferred to the workplace. It is one of the most effective techniques to use for adult learners.

Geo people involved right from the start. It is important to engage participants from the very beginning of a training session, especially mangers who may be resenting the time away from work and rolling their eyes at "yet another" required training seminar. Icebreakers can help break down such attitudes and ultimately achieve better training outcomes for all concerned. Icebreakers are short, fun exercises that require audience participation. Icebreakers should be designed to test the participants' knowledge of subject matter while at the same time setting an upbeat tone for the training. Icebreakers can help people feel more comfortable and get to know one another and start a training session off with energy and enthusiasm. In order to be most effective, icebreakers should relate to the training topic.

Use case studies. Case studies can be very helpful in getting the material across in practical terms. One method of tailoring training to your audience is to survey managers in advance of the training and ask for worst-case scenarios. The case studies can then be based on responses from the participants. In order to get the most from the use of case studies, have participants review the case study and be prepared to response to such questions as these:

- What are the perspectives, assumptions, and feelings of the different people in this situation? Working through these issues from the different viewpoints of supervisor and employee can be very useful in training managers in conflict resolution skills.

- What are the probable outcomes if this situation is not addressed effectively? Will the problem continue to arise? Will productivity or morale suffer? Is litigation likely?

- What is the least effective and most effective way to handle this situation? At the time of the incident: in public/in private? After the incident: in public/in private?

- What factors helped create this situation? What could be done to prevent this type of situation in the future?

Use questions to get them involved. Questions from the participants are an important part of every training session; they provide feedback and a method of gauging whether the participants understand the material. Trainers typically state at the start of a session that questions are welcome and then stop periodically and directly ask for questions.

One way to encourage questions is to assign a group of participants in advance to work together to come up with questions. You could also designate a message board or flip chart for questions. Participants write questions on notes and post them on the board, and you retrieve them during a break. This avoids the problem of participants who are too shy to speak up during the session.

How you respond to the first question can make a big impression and can discourage further questions if not handled properly. Is your tone and attitude open and welcoming, or do you convey the impression that you view questions as an interruption? Be sure to respond in a helpful way, repeating the question so that everyone in the room can follow your answer. Then state your appreciation and compliment the person on his or her question.

Time your training for maximum effectiveness. When planning classroom-based training, most experts now agree that training should not be conducted over several days. It is more effective if employees can attend the training, practice what they have learned on the job, and return to the next session with questions before moving on to the next block of training. Retention is better, and employees stay more focused, if the training is for shorter periods of time, such as 4-hour blocks, over a few weeks rather than given all at once. Otherwise, employees tend to get overloaded and fail to apply the learning once they return to work.

Breaking Through Language Barriers

As more and more non-English speaking workers join the workforce, ensuring that the non-English speaking employees in your company understand and can implement training is critical to your organization's success. Here are some strategies.

Use native speakers as trainers. Training for Hispanics and other non- English speaking employees has traditionally been limited to an Anglo speaker with a translator in front of the class. Much can be lost in the translation. If at all possible, provide trainers who are native speakers. Keep class size small, and encourage student participation.

Be aware of cultural differences. Cultural differences often interfere with training outcomes. For example, workers from some cultural backgrounds may be reluctant to disobey work orders, even if unsafe or potentially deadly, out of a sense of duty or respect for authority. Sexual harassment training might be problematic for female employees of certain religious backgrounds who would be reluctant to confront a harasser directly. You will want to take into account such potential differences in planning and conducting training.

Provide hands-on training. Paper-and-pen tests are ineffective for a worker population with limited education and literacy. Instead, use a hands- on approach where no written tests are required, and content is taught through an actual live demonstration.

New Employee Orientation and Training

Because orientation is generally a worker's introduction to your organization, it's important to do it well. Properly introducing and assimilating new employees into the company will have a real effect on the job they do in the future. In fact, studies show that the impressions a new worker forms during the first weeks on the job have a significant impact— positive or negative—on long-range performance and job satisfaction. Orientation is where most of these first impressions are formed.

Orientation Basics

During orientation, a new employee needs to learn basic information about your company and the new job.

1. There are six main objectives of new employee orientation:

2. To welcome new employees on board and make them feel comfortable

3. To facilitate adjustment to the job. The sink or swim method of introducing employees to a new job is counterproductive and may permanently damage the employee's relationship with you, the job, and the company. A good orientation program conveys all the initial information employees need to know about their jobs during the first few weeks.

4. To acquaint new workers with the company—its mission, its market, its operation, and its people.

5. To inform new employees about a broad range of company policies that affect all aspects of their work and their relationship with the organization.

6. To complete required paperwork—all the forms and documents that must be completed during the first few days on the job.

To open the channels of communication through which employees can obtain information, ask questions, and discuss job problems. You will rely on effective two-way communication not only during the orientation process but also throughout your professional relationship with an employee.

Although you will not be involved in all phases of new employee orientation, you are key to making the process successful. Supervisors need training, as well as your support, in order to get this critical process right. Use the information in this section to train supervisors and get those new hires off to a great start.

Suggested Orientation Schedule

Orientation should not be done all at once on the employee's first day at work, but should happen over a period of weeks as part of the new employee's progress toward maximum productivity and to provide an ongoing check on how much the employee is learning as well as what problems he or she is experiencing.

First day. The following activities should be at the top of the list for the first day of a new employee's orientation:

- **Welcome.** Supervisors should be sure to welcome new employees personally and let them know that the company is glad to have them on board.

- **Introductions and workplace tour.** New employees should meet at least some of their co-workers and get a tour of the facility, including the locker room, cafeteria, vending machines, restrooms, and so on.

- **Paperwork.** Supervisors should make sure the employee has time at some point to complete any paperwork that must be turned into Human Resources that day or the next morning.

- **Keys, equipment, etc.** This is the time to issue any keys, equipment, parking passes, badges, or other items the employee will need.

- **Job description.** Supervisors should take time to sit down with new employees and be as specific about duties and responsibilities as possible. They should review the job description and describe a typical day on the job. They should also explain the importance of the position and how it fits into the operation as a whole.

- **Expectations.** Supervisors need to talk to new employees about their expectations and performance standards. They need to explain how performance will be monitored and evaluated. They should also outline the critical skills needed on the job and establish priorities.

- **Department procedures.** Important department procedures should be reviewed on the first day, including how to record time worked, calling in sick, and safety procedures.

- **Questions.** Supervisors should take the time to answer the employee's questions as they go along. There is a lot of information to take in all at once, and new employees need to be assured that everything will be reviewed in the days ahead.

- **Job assignment.** It is also important to assign a meaningful task. A first work assignment that will get the employee involved in the job needs to be integrated into the day. It can be something simple like watching and helping a co-worker perform a task the new employee will be doing, reviewing files from the previous jobholder, or becoming familiar with a piece of equipment.

- **Lunch.** The supervisor should either personally have lunch with the new employee or have an employee in the department take the new employee to lunch.

- **End of the shift.** It's important to end the day on a positive note. Before the employee leaves at the end of the shift, the supervisor should spend some private time with the employee to review progress made on the first-day work assignment and answer all additional questions. If at all possible, touch base with the new hire yourself at the end of the day.

Second day. On the second day, the supervisor can continue with any items left over from the first day. The supervisor can also get started with more in-depth job training. The new employee can also begin another job assignment to be completed with the help and guidance of an experienced co-worker.

- **End of the first week.** By the end of the first week, job training should be well under way. The new employee should be familiar with the main orientation information and have had time to complete all necessary documentation. The employee should also have become more familiar with the job, the department, co-workers, and the larger facility. At the end of the first week, supervisors should schedule a formal meeting with the employee to make sure that he or she is adjusting to the job well. At that time, the supervisor can review the employee's understanding of duties, responsibilities, procedures, and so forth. This meeting will also provide the employee with a chance to ask questions and for the supervisor to clarify and misconceptions about the job.

- **After 2 weeks.** The supervisor should meet formally with the employee again to discuss progress and answer questions. This gives the supervisor the opportunity to check on how well the employee is doing with job training and to discuss any problems concerning training or other aspects of the job.

- **After 4 weeks.** The formal orientation period will pretty much have run its course by this time. At this time supervisors can give new employees a brief evaluation of their performance, identifying areas of strength and needed growth. This is a good time to review the performance appraisal process so that the new employee knows what to expect from the first review. Supervisors can also take this opportunity to discuss future training needs with the employee.

Basic Training for New Supervisors

Imagine being promoted to supervisor after a few months on the job, required to complete reports for weekly meetings that might as well have been in another language, and thrown into the job of supervisor with little guidance. Unfortunately, this scenario is fairly typical. Employers promote employees on the basis of their technical expertise—not on their leadership skills—and often don't teach them how to adapt to their new supervisory role. Both employer and employee can be disappointed when new managers don't live up to expectations. Worse still, new supervisors can make potentially costly mistakes. This "baptism by fire" approach can lead to poor results that may affect the company's bottom line and cause problems with employee morale, turnover, or even lawsuits if an untrained supervisor runs afoul of employment laws while conducting a job interview.

When to Train

If top performers are to become top managers, they need a formal training program. One critical element of an effective training program is the timing of the training. The amount and type of training are also important.

If new managers get too much information too soon, the training will not be absorbed. If too little attention is paid at the outset, serious mistakes could be made. Anyone who has been through week-long training session knows that it is difficult to stay focused and recall the material once back on the job. Companies can get better results by conducting training for new managers for no more than a day at a time and then allowing managers to go back to work and apply what they have learned right away.

The material should also be offered in small increments, offering short instruction time and the opportunity for new managers to practice their new skills. Follow-up discussions about what new methods were effective on the job can also be helpful. And follow-up training can be targeted toward specific areas in which a new supervisor may be having trouble, such as delegation of tasks. Training is often wasted if it is not tied into things new supervisors deal within day-to-day operations.

What Subjects to Train About

Like most other training, new supervisor training must be based on the business objectives of the company.

The first phase of instruction for new managers should focus on skills they will need in the first 90 days, minimizing the risk that they will make early mistakes and lose credibility. Certain basic personnel material and business strategy should be covered immediately, while the leadership skills and other more developmental aspects of manager training can be handled later.

The following items should be covered when training new supervisors. Don't try to do this all in one session, however! Remember that training is most effective when done in a series that allows ample time for questioning, interacting, and practicing the new skills.

- **Understanding legal and union contract information.** New supervisors need a comprehensive course in federal and state employment laws 9see the suggested topic like in the second section of this chapter). In a unionized environment, employees may never have become familiar with their own union agreement. As supervisors, they need to know the proper disciplinary procedures to follow to avoid grievances. Since you're going it alone, don't hesitate to ask the union representatives to help you with this type of training.

- **Interviewing applicants.** Many new supervisors may be required to hire new employees, yet they have no experience with the legalities of interviewing or with the fine art of matching applicants to the right jobs. When training in these skills, role-plays and mock interviews can be a big help. Having a new supervisor sit in on an interview done by one of your most experienced supervisors could also be beneficial. Of course, legal issues faced during the hiring process need to be reinforced.

- **Adjusting to the new role of supervisor in relation to former co- workers.** New managers should be prepared for the fact that their relationships with their former peers will change. Conducting a training session with both new and experienced supervisors—those who also came up through the ranks—can be a great way for new supervisors to hear how others have handled this sometime sticky problem.

- **Delegating.** As top performers, many new managers have difficulty letting go of the temptation to do the work and must learn to rely on subordinates to get the job done. When those sub-ordinates used to be co-workers, they may find it especially difficult to delegate. Help them see that delegating not only frees up their time for their new tasks, but it also gives their team members a chance to shine as they succeed at new duties.

- **Providing constructive feedback.** Many managers—both new ones and experienced ones—avoid giving employees corrective feedback. Confronting employees' behavior can be unpleasant and can cause the employee to react negatively. Rather than face these consequences, managers often procrastinate or ignore poor performance. Help new supervisors see that the better practice is to correct small problems as they come up, rather than wait until an employee becomes a disciplinary problem. Training for supervisors in this area should be designed around their real-life problems on the job. After learning the basics on how to give feedback, the participants can spend the remaining time role-play scenarios in which they practice giving corrective e feedback. This should provide supervisors with enough confidence to return to work ready to give regular feedback.

- **Managing performance.** New supervisors have seen your performance management only from one side of the desk. Now they will be in charge of writing and delivering performance reviews. Along with training on giving constructive feedback, you need to provide new supervisors with the nuts and bolts of your company's performance management system.

- **Leadership skills.** Most new supervisors have been hired for the job, or promoted into it, because management saw leadership potential in them. Even so, almost all supervisors can benefit from leadership training to reinforce their innate tendencies and help them learn how to motivate others. (Refer to the section on Leadership in Chapter 2 for more on this training topic.)

Among the critical legal topics you will want to train supervisors on are:

- Age Discrimination in Employment Act (ADEA)
- Americans with Disabilities Act (ADA)
- Basic wage and salary issues
- Discrimination
- Documentation and recordkeeping
- Employee benefits
- Employee Retirement and Income Security Act (ERISA)

- Employee rights
- Employees' privacy rights
- Fair Labor Standards Act (FLSA)
- Family and Medical Leave Act (FMLA)
- Health Insurance Portability and Accountability Act (HIPAA)
- Legal issues in firing
- Legal issues in hiring
- Performance management and performance review
- Sexual harassment

Making Training Stick

One of the hardest things for new supervisors to grasp is that the rules have changed. No longer are they judged on their efforts alone. Now, their success or failure as a supervisor also depends on the success or failure of their team. If you start off your training sessions by introducing that concept, you are bound to have a room full of people paying careful attention to you!

To ensure that new supervisors take their training to heart, help them realize that they will now be evaluated on how well they manage the performance of the people they supervise.

Finally, evaluate the training, with the input of the new supervisors, to help you plan refresher courses and to be sure that your training efforts evolve along with the company's priorities.

Evaluating the Effectiveness of Training

Evaluation should not just focus on how participants responded to the program and on how their knowledge, skill levels, and behavior on the job have actually changed. While it may be difficult, it is essential to isolate the effects of training—in other words, to determine that change has come about because of training and not for some other reason.

Among the factors you should evaluate are:

- How applicable the training was to the employee's job
- Whether the employee was given adequate opportunities to practice newly acquired skills or to learn through examples
- Whether there was sufficient opportunity to ask questions and discuss training content with other trainees
- If there was an instructor, how qualified he or she was to present the training materials
- How the employee reacted to the training and perceived that it was improving his or her knowledge and skill level
- The extent to which the employee was able to apply the newly acquired skills or knowledge to the job.
- The impact of training on the company's business
- How enthusiastically the employee would recommend the training to a co-worker

Proving Return on Investment

These days, HR and training professionals are being asked to demonstrate the value of training with hard data. Return on investment (ROI) analysis is one form of evaluation that attempts to measure the effectiveness of training, typically in financial terms. Dr. Donald Kirkpatrick's four levels of evaluating ROI for training have been in use for over 40 years.

Level I refers to the students' evaluation of the training, usually in the form of an evaluation sheet.

Level II involves conducting pretests and/or posttests to determine that learning has actually taken place.

Level III evaluates whether the learning is actually being applied in the workplace.

Level IV involves determining that the company is actually realizing business results from the learning.

Level IV typically requires calculating the tangible and intangible costs and benefits of the training. As in any analysis, the benefits must exceed the costs to consider the training successful.

When the economy was booming and companies were willing to assume that training was beneficial, training evaluation forms and post-testing (Levels I and II) were enough. However, in today's business climate—with tight training budgets and much speculation about the actual value of training—proof of training retention and actual business benefit is required (Levels III and IV). So how do you go about proving Levels III and IV or ROI?

Level III asks whether participants apply what they learned in training to their job. The best people to observe whether training is actually applied are managers and supervisors of the trainees. The managers and supervisors must be thoroughly trained in the evaluation system and need to establish a system for leveling out the inconsistencies between observers' judgments.

Level IV asks: "Did this on-the-job application produce measurable results?" These results may include increases in productivity and efficiency, decreases in absenteeism and occupational accidents, and a lessening of customer complaints. Isolating the effects of training from other variables that produce an effect in these areas, either through statistics or by using a control group, is vital to getting a clear picture of ROI.

Conducting a Cost-Benefit Analysis

How do you prove the "worth" of training? Try a simple cost-benefit analysis. Among the costs of training are supplies, refreshments, advertising, rentals or purchases of needed equipment, facility usage, and the cost of an outside trainer (if applicable), as well as the cost of your trainees' missing work.

To calculate the total benefits, you must evaluate the tangible results of training and assign a monetary value to the so-called "hard-benefits," which include the following:

- Increased productivity (units produced, items sold, forms processed, tasks completed)

- Improved quality (less waste, less rework of product, fewer defects)
- Reduced turnover
- Reduction in lost-time injuries
- Reduction in workers' compensation insurance claims
- Increased customer satisfaction as reflected in increased repeat sales

In addition, consider the "soft benefits" of improved communication, enhanced corporate image, improved conflict resolution, improved morale, and increased loyalty. One way to approximate the value of soft benefits is to ask individuals within your organization to give a monetary figure for these intangibles. Talk to employees, managers, supervisors, and executives, and then take an average of the numbers that give you.

Finally, to build a training effort that adds value to the bottom line instead of decreasing it, HR must measure efficacy. You need to ask participants if the programs helped them perform their jobs better— and how. You also need to find out from supervisors if your training program has helped achieve their units' business goals.

As you can see, training that passes the cost-benefits analysis is training that is aligned with your company's strategy or business initiatives. That means that you must be a full partner with the management team. Without that partnership, your training efforts will fall short.

Training & Development

Training is a process of learning a sequence of programmed behavior. It improves the employee's performance on the current job and prepares them for an intended job.

Development not only improves job performance but also brings about the growth of the personality. Individuals not only mature regarding their potential capacities but also become better individuals.

Difference between Training & Development: Training:

1. It's a short term process

2. Refers to instruction in technical and mechanical problems

3. Targeted in most cases for non-managerial personnel

4. Specific job related purpose

Development:

1. It is a long term educational process.

2. Refers to philosophical and theoretical educational concepts

3. Managerial personnel

4. General knowledge purpose

Purpose of Training:

1. To improve Productivity: Training leads to increased operational productivity and increased company profit.

2. To improve Quality: Better trained workers are less likely to make operational mistakes.

3. To improve Organizational Climate: Train leads to improved production and product quality which enhances financial incentives. This in turn increases the overall morale of the organization.

4. To increase Health and Safety: Proper training prevents industrial accidents.

5. Personal Growth: Training gives employees a wider awareness, an enlarged skill base and that leads to enhanced personal growth.

Steps in Training Process:

1. Discovering or Identifying Training needs: A training program is designed to assist in providing solutions for specific operational problems or to improve performance of a trainee.

- *Organizational determination and analysis:* Allocation of resources that relate to organizational goal.

- *Operational Analysis:* Determination of a specific employee behavior required for a particular task.

- *Man Analysis:* Knowledge, attitude and skill one must possess for attainment of organizational objectives.

2. Getting ready for the job: The trainer has to be prepared for the job. And also who needs to be trained—the newcomer or the existing employee or the supervisory staff.

3. Preparation of the learner:

- Putting the learner at ease

- Stating the importance and ingredients of the job

- Creating interest

- Placing the learner as close to his normal working position

- Familiarizing him with the equipment, materials and trade terms

4. Preparation of Operation and Knowledge: The trainer should clearly tell, show, illustrate and question in order to convey the new knowledge and operations. The trainee should be encouraged to ask questions in order to indicate that he really knows and understands the job.

5. Performance Try out: The trainee is asked to go through the job several times. This gradually builds up skill, speed and confidence.

6. Follow-up: This evaluates the effectiveness of the entire training effort. The Sequence of Training Program can be put in a Flowchart as below:

Discovering or Identifying Training Needs—>Getting Ready for the job

—>Preparation of Learner (Creating desire)—>Presentation of Operation & Knowledge—>Performance Try out—>Follow up and Evaluation

Training Techniques

An effective training fulfills the following criteria:

1. Adaptation of the technique/method to the learner and the job

2. Provides motivation to the trainee to improve job performance

3. Creates trainee's active participation in the learning process

4. Provide knowledge of results about attempts to improve

Creating Training Stickiness Before the Employee Training Sessions

You can do the following in advance of the employee training session to increase the likelihood that the training you do will actually transfer to the workplace.

- **Make sure the need is a training and development opportunity.** Do thorough needs and skills analysis to determine the real need for employee training and development. Make sure the opportunity you are pursuing or the problem you are solving is a training issue.

If the employee is failing in some aspect of her/her job, determine whether you have provided the employee with the time and tools needed to perform the job. Does the employee clearly understand what is expected from him or her on the job? Ask yourself whether the employee has the temperament and talent necessary for his/her current position; consider whether the job is a good skill, ability, and interest fit?

- **Create a context for the employee training and development.** Provide information for the employee about why the new skills, skill enhancement, or information is necessary. Make certain the employee understands the link between the training and his job.

You can enhance the impact of the training even further if the employee sees the link between the training and his ability to contribute to the accomplishment of the organization's business plan and goals. It's also important to provide rewards and recognition as a result of successful completion and application of the training. (People like completion certificates, for instance. One company I worked for a short time lists employee names and completed training sessions in the company newsletter.) This contextual information will help create an attitude of motivation as the employee attends the training. It will assist the employee to want to look for relevant information to apply after the session.

- **Provide training and development that is really relevant to the skill you want the employee to attain** or the information he needs to expand his work horizons. You may need to design an employee training session internally if nothing from training providers exactly meets your needs. Or, seek out providers who are willing to customize their offerings to match your specific needs.

It is ineffective to ask an employee to attend a training session on general communication when his immediate need is to learn how to provide feedback in a way that minimizes defensive behavior. The employee will regard the training session as mostly a waste of time or too basic; his complaints will invalidate potential learning.

Whenever possible, connect the employee training to the employee's job and work objectives. If you work in an organization that invests in a self- development component in the appraisal process, make sure the connection to the plan is clear.

- **Favor employee training and development that has measurable objectives and specified outcomes** that will transfer back to the job. Design or obtain employee training that has clearly stated objectives with measurable outcomes. Ascertain that the content leads the employee to attaining the skill or information promised in the objectives.

The following will help you provide training and development that will transfer skills back to the job.

- **Provide information for the employee about exactly what the training session will involve,** prior to the training. Explain what is expected of the employee at the training session. This will help reduce the person's normal anxiety about trying something new. If he/she knows what to expect, he/she can focus on the learning and training transfer rather than his/her potential discomfort with the unknown.

(When you offer a team building session, as an example, people invariably will ask you if they will have to touch each other or "do hugs." They don't, but this really drives home the point for you about letting people know what to expect prior to attending the session.)

- Make clear to the employee that the **training is his/her responsibility and he/she needs to take the employee training** seriously. He/she is expected to apply him/herself to the employee training and development process before, during, and after the session. This includes completing pre-training assignments, actively participating in the session, and applying new ideas and skills upon returning to work.

- Make sure that internal or external training provides **supply pre-training assignments.** Reading or thought-provoking exercises in advance of the session promote thoughtful consideration of the training content. Exercises or self-assessments, provided and scored in advance of the session, save precious training time for interaction and new information. These ideas will engage the employee in thinking about the subject of the session prior to the training day. This supplies important paybacks in terms of his interest, commitment, and involvement.

- **Train supervisors and managers either first or simultaneously so they know and understand the skills** and information provided in the training session. This will allow the supervisor to model the appropriate behavior and learning provide and environment in which the employee can apply the training, and create the clear expectation that he/she expects to see different behavior or thinking as a result of the training. An executive, who has participated in the same training as the rest of the organization, is a powerful role model when he/she is observed applying the training.

- **Train managers and supervisors in their role in the training process.** The average supervisor has rarely experienced effective training during his/her career. Even more rare is the supervisor who has worked in an environment that maximize transfer of training to the actual workplace. Thus it is a mistake to believe that supervisors automatically know what must happen for effective training to take place.

- **You can coach supervisors about their role.** Provide a handy tip sheet that explains in detail the organization's expectations of the supervisor in support of effective training. At one General Motors location, the education and training staff provided a three-hour class called The Organization and the Training Process. The session was most effective in communicating roles and responsibilities to supervisory staff.

- **Ask Supervisors to meet with employees prior to the training session** to accomplish all I have recommended in this book. Discuss with the individual what he/she hopes to learn in the session. Discuss any concerns he/she may have about applying the training in the work environment. Determine if key learning points are important for the organization in return for the investment of his/her time in the training. Identify any obstacles the employee may expect to experience as he/she transfers the training to the workplace.

Development

Management development attempts to improve managerial performance by imparting

1. Knowledge
2. Changing attitudes
3. Increasing skills

The major objective of development is managerial effectiveness through a planned and a deliberate process of learning. This provides for a planned growth of managers to meet the future organizational needs.

Development Process:

1. Setting Development Objectives: It develops a framework from which executive need can be determined.

2. Ascertaining Development Needs: It aims at organizational planning & Forecast the present and future growth.

3. Determining Development Needs: This consists of

- Appraisal of present management talent
- Management Manpower Inventory

The above two process will determine the skill deficiencies that are relative to the future needs of the organization.

1. Conducting Development Programs: It is carried out on the basis of needs of different individuals, differences in their attitudes and behavior, also their physical, intellectual and emotional qualities. Thus a comprehensive and well-conceived program is prepared depending on the organizational needs and the time and cost involved.

2. Program Evaluation: It is an attempt to assess the value of training in order to achieve organizational objectives.

The Development process can be pictorially represented in a Flowchart as below:

Setting Development Objectives->Ascertaining Development Needs->Determining Development Needs->Conducting Development Program->Program Evaluation

CHAPTER FIVE

EMPLOYEE RETENTION & CONFLICT RESOLUTION IN THE WORKPLACE

An effective manager pays attention to many facets of management, leadership and learning within organizations. So, it's difficult to take the topic of "management success" and say that the following ten items are the most important for management success. I will, however, suggest seven management success skills without which I don't believe you can be a successful manager.

The most important issue in management success is being a person that others want to follow. Every action you take during your career in an organization helps determine whether people will one day want to follow you.

A successful manager, one whom others want to follow:

- Builds effective and responsive **interpersonal relationships.** Reporting staff members, colleagues and executives respect his or her ability to demonstrate caring, collaboration, respect, trust and attentiveness.

- **Communicates effectively** in person, print and email. Listening and two-way feedback characterize his or her interaction with others.

- **Builds the team** and enables other staff to collaborate more effectively with each other. People feel they have become more—more effective, more creative, more productive—in the presence of a team builder.

- **Understands the financial aspects** of the business and sets goals and measures and documents staff progress and success.

- Knows how to create an environment in which people experience **positive morale and recognition** and employees are motivated to work hard for the success of the business.

- **Leads by example** and provides recognition when others do the same.

- **Helps people grow and develop** their skills and capabilities through education and on-the-job learning.

Your expectations of people and their expectations of themselves are the key factors in how well people perform at work. Known as the Pygmalion effect, respectively, the power of expectations cannot be overestimated. These are the fundamental principles you can apply to performance expectations and potential performance improvement at work.

You can summarize the Pygmalion effect, often known as the power of expectations, by considering:

- Every supervisor has expectations of the people who report to him.

- Supervisors communicate these expectations consciously or unconsciously.

- People pick up on, or consciously or unconsciously read, these expectations from their supervisor.

- People perform in ways that are consistent with the expectations they have picked up on from the supervisor.

The Pygmalion effect was described by J. Sterling Livingston in the September/October 1988 Harvard Business Review. "The way managers treat their subordinates is subtly influenced by what they expect of them," Livingston said in his article, Pygmalion in Management.

The Pygmalion effect enables staff to excel in response to the manager's message that they are capable of success and expected to succeed. The Pygmalion effect can also undermine staff performance when the subtle communication from the manager tells them the opposite. These cues are often subtle. As an example, the supervisor fails to praise a staff person's performance as frequently as he praises others. The supervisor talks less to a particular employee.

Livingston went on to say about the supervisor, "If he is unskilled, he leaves scars on the careers of the young men (and women), cuts deeply into their self-esteem and distorts their image of themselves as human beings. But if he is skillful and has high expectations of his subordinates, their self- confidence will grow, their capabilities will develop and their productivity will be high. More often than he realizes, the manager is Pygmalion."

Can you imagine how performance will improve if your supervisors communicate positive thoughts about people to people? If the supervisor actually believes that every employee has the ability to make a positive contribution at work, the telegraphing of that message, either consciously or unconsciously, will positively affect employee performance.

And, the effect of the supervisor gets even better than this. When the supervisor holds positive expectations about people, she helps individuals improve their self-concept ant thus, self-esteem. People believe they can succeed and contribute and their performance rises to the level of their own expectations.

Great managers break every rule perceived as "conventional wisdom," when dealing with the selection, motivation, and development of staff. So state Marcus Buckingham and Curt Coffman in First Break All The Rules: What the World's Greatest Managers Do Differently, a book which presents the findings of the Gallup organization's interviews with over 80,000 successful managers.

Most powerful about these findings about successful management is that each "great" manager was identified based upon the performance results he produced in his organization. Here are some of the key ideas discussed in the great managers' book.

Additionally, I'll expand upon the human resource management and development information from the book with specific examples and recommendations. Managers and human resource management and development professionals can apply the research findings to jump start their management career success.

An Overall New Approach to Human Resource Development

The insight most commonly expressed during the interviews with 90,000 great managers challenges traditional human resource management and development beliefs. Thousands of great managers stated variations on this belief: "People don't change that much. Don't waste time trying to put in what was left out. Try to draw out what was left in. That is hard enough."

The implications of this insight for training and performance development are profound. This insight encourages building on what people can already do well instead of trying to "fix" weaker talents and abilities. The traditional performance improvement process identifies specific, average or below performance areas. Suggestions for improvement, either verbal or in a formal appraisal process focus on developing these weaknesses.

As an example, if I employ a person who lacks people skills, a diverse group of staff members can form a customer service team that includes him. Other employees with excellent people skills make his weakness less evident. And, the organization is able to capitalize on his product knowledge when dealing with product quality issues.

Does this mean that great managers never help people improve their inadequate skills, knowledge, or methods? No, but they shift their emphasis to human resource development in areas in which the employee already has talent, knowledge, and skills.

The Four Vital Jobs for Great Managers

Buckingham and Coffman identify four twists on conventional approaches which further define the differences in tactics espoused by great managers.

- Select people based on talent.
- When setting expectations for employees, establish the right outcomes.
- When motivating an individual, focus on strengths.
- To develop an individual, find the right job fit for the person.

Select people Based on Talent

During the Gallup interviews, great managers stated that they selected staff members based on talent, rather than experience, education, or intelligence. Gallup defined "talents" by studying the talents needed to achieve in 150 distinct roles. Talents identified are:

- **striving**—(examples: drive for achievement, need for expertise, drive to put beliefs in action),

- **thinking**—(examples: focus, discipline, personal responsibility), and

- **relating**—(examples: empathy, attentiveness to individual differences, ability to persuade, and taking charge).

Human Resource professionals will support line managers more effectively if they recommend methods for identifying talents such as realistic testing and behavioral interviewing. When checking background, look for patterns of talent application. (As an example, did the candidate develop every new position he/she ever obtained from scratch?)

Want the bottom line when it comes to employee retention? **The quality of the supervision an employee receives is critical to employee retention.** People leave managers and supervisors more often than they leave companies or jobs.

It is not enough that the manager is well-liked or a nice person. Sure, a nice, likeable manager earns you some points with your employees. A draconian, nasty, or controlling manager takes points away from your organization. So will below market benefits and compensation. But, a manager or supervisor, who is a pro at employee retention, knows that the quality of the supervision is the key factor in employee retention.

Effective Managers Create Employee Retention

Managers who retain staff start by communicating clear expectations to the employee. They share their picture of what constitutes success for the employee in both the expected deliverables from and the performance of their job.

These managers provide frequent feedback and make the employee feel valued. When an employee completes an exchange with a manager who retains staff, he or she feels empowered, enabled, and confident in their ability to get the job done.

Employee complaints about managers and supervisors center on these areas. Employees leave managers who fail to:

- provide clarity about expectations,
- provide clarity about career development and earning potential,
- give regular feedback about performance,
- hold scheduled meetings, and
- provide a framework within which the employee perceives he can succeed.

How to Help Managers With Employee Retention

Almost every manager can increase his/her ability to retain employees by developing his/her management skills. Teaching a manager about how to value people can be more challenging. Particularly if the manager doesn't already value people and their contributions in his/her mind and heart, it will be a leap for his/her to change his/her values.

These ideas will help your organization develop managers who believe in and act in ways that support employee retention.

- Integrate core values about people and a mission and vision that enable people to align themselves with the company direction. Communicate the importance of these, and clear expectations about the behaviors expected from managers to accomplish these, to every manager.
- Negotiate a performance development plan and each manager that stresses the expected managerial areas of development
- Provide training in core management skills to every manager. Core management skills include how to:
- Integrate performance management including goal setting,
- Give and receive feedback,

- Recognize and value employees,

- Coach employee performance,

- Handle employee complaints and problems,

- Provide a motivating work environment, and

- Hold career development discussions with employees.

- Hold regular meetings to provide management development coaching and feedback. You can assist managers to improve their management style and skills. A regular meeting helps you debrief events as they occur, while memories of the exchanges are fresh in the manager's mind.

- Schedule and hold learning organization events such as book clubs, product training, project debriefs, and discussion and planning meetings.

- Provide funding for conferences and educational development opportunities for managers to continue learning.

- As part of a fully integrated performance management system, provide 360 degree feedback so managers know how their management style is perceived.

What if a Manager Fails at Employee Retention?

If a manager fails at employee retention, the chances are good that the manager has been unable or unwilling to develop their ability to manage and value people across the board. Managers who exhibit a pattern in which their key employees leave your organization cannot retain their management role.

If you have fairly and ethically provided the manager the learning opportunities suggested here, you can, in good conscience, remove the individual from the managerial role. My experience has been that most managers consider this is such a loss of prestige and "face" that they voluntarily leave the organization.

If they choose to stay, however, they must commit to being effective, contributing employees. If the manager cannot make this leap, you will need to let the manager go before their negativity impacts the rest of your workplace.

Give the management development opportunities listed here; most managers will be able to become managers who retain their best employees. Your investment in your managers can fuel your organization's ongoing success. After all, it is the quality of the people you employ and retain that is the heart of your business success.

You can make their day or break their day. Your choice. No kidding. Other than the decisions individuals make on their own about liking their work, you are the most powerful factor in employee motivation and morale.

As a manager or supervisor, your impact on employee motivation is immeasurable. By your works, your body language, and the expression on your face, as a manager, supervisor, or leader, you telegraph your opinion of their value to the people you employ.

Feeling valued by their supervisor in the workplace is key to high employee motivation and morale. Feeling valued ranks right up there for most people with liking the work, competitive pay, opportunities for training and advancement, and feeling "in" on the latest news.

Building high employee motivation and morale is both challenging and yet supremely simple. Building high employee motivation and morale requires that you pay attention every day to profoundly meaningful aspects of your impact on life at work.

Your Arrival at Work Sets the Employee Motivation Tone for the Day

Picture Mr. Stressed-Out and Grumpy. He arrives at work with a frown on his face. His body language telegraphs "over-worked" and unhappy. He move slowly and treats the first person who approaches him abruptly. It takes only a few minutes for the entire workplace to get the word. Stay away from Mr. Stressed-Out and Grumpy if you know what's good for you this morning.

Your arrival and the first moments you spend with staff each day have an immeasurable impact on positive employee motivation and morale. Start the day right. Smile. Walk tall and confidently. Walk around your workplace and greet people. Share the goals and expectations for the day. Let the staff know that today is going to be a great day. It starts with you. You can make their day.

Use Simple, Powerful Words for Employee Motivation

Sometimes in my work, I get gifts. I recently interviewed an experienced supervisor for a position open at a client company. He/she indicated that he/she was popular with the people at his/her former company as evidenced by employees wanting to work on his/her shift.

Responding to my question, he/she said that part of his/her success was that he/she liked and appreciated people. He/she sent the right message. He/she also uses simple, powerful, motivational words to demonstrate he/she values people. He/she says "please" and "thank you" and "you're doing a good job." How often do you take the time to use these simple, powerful words, and others like them, in your interaction with staff? You can make their day.

Provide Regular Feedback for Employee Motivation

When I poll supervisors, the motivation and morale builder they identify first is knowing how they are doing at work. Your staff members need the same information. They want to know when they have done a project well and when you are disappointed in their results. They need this information as soon as possible following the event.

They need to work with you to make sure they produce a positive outcome the next time. Set up a daily or weekly schedule and make sure feedback happens. You'll be surprised how effective this tool can be in building employee motivation and morale. You can make their day.

For Employee Motivation, Make Sure People Know What You Expect

In the best book I've read on the subject, Why Employees Don't Do What They're Supposed to Do and What to Do about It, by Ferdinand Fournies, setting clear expectations is often a supervisor's first failure. Supervisors think they have clearly stated work objectives, numbers needed report deadlines and requirements, but the employee received a different message.

Or, the requirements change in the middle of the day, job, or project.

While the new expectations are communicated—usually poorly— the reason for the change or the context for the change is rarely discussed.

This causes staff members to think that the company leaders don't know what they are doing. This is hardly a confidence, morale-building feeling.

This is bad news for employee motivation and morale. Make sure you get feedback from the employee so you know he understands what you need.

Share the goals and reasons for doing the task or project. In a manufacturing environment, don't emphasize just numbers if you want a quality product finished quickly. If you must make a change midway through a task or a project, tell the staff why the change is needed; tell them everything you know. You can make their day.

Provide Regular Feedback for Employee Motivation

When I poll supervisors, the motivation and morale builder they identify first is knowing how they are doing at work. Your staff members need the same information. They want to know when they have done a project well and when you are disappointed in their results. They need this information as soon as possible following the event.

They need to work with you to make sure they produce a positive outcome the next time. Set up a daily or weekly schedule and make sure feedback happens. You'll be surprised how effective this tool can be in building employee motivation and morale. You can make their day.

Use these work relationship tips, leadership tips, and management tips to become an effective, successful employee, business leader, and/ or management professional. These work success and happiness tips, leadership tips, and management tips convey best workplace and business leadership and management practices.

These work success and happiness tips, leadership tips, and management tips are classified by topic for your convenience in accessing information. Use these tips as your personal workplace, leadership, and management coaching resource.

These work success and happiness tips, leadership tips, and management tips are classified by topic for your convenience in accessing information. Use these tips as your personal workplace, leadership, and management coaching resource.

Never lose sight of the need for profitability in your business. Yes, your business likely exists for additional reasons, too. Some of you love the work you do. Others feel your organization's mission is exciting and fulfilling. But the fundamental reason a business exists is to make a profit. Without a profit, you can't support employees and their families; you can't sustain the business. A client company lost sight of this fact recently. The company sold several of its products for less money than the total cost of parts purchased plus labor and shipping. Why? Because the company needed to develop the measurement system necessary to project profitability before parts were purchased. With these metrics in place, profitability is assured.

As businesses grow activity needed is recruiting, of course. But, additionally, people must be paid and people need benefits. So, often, the first person holding part of an HR role is the person who pays the staff. And this person generally reports to finance and accounting. Just because this is how a small business usually grows, doesn't make it the right path for your business to travel. It's not.

Every organization needs checks and balances. HR reporting to finance ties the hands of the people most likely to advocate for effective people policies and organization development, your HR staff. HR reporting to finance moves your HR person one step further away from where organizational decision making is occurring. When HR reports to finance, policy decisions are likely to be primarily finance driven and often not people friendly. Keep your check and balance in place. HR should never report to finance and accounting.

If another example, a new employee was asked to send out a note with a question and a deadline to the Director—VP level managers in her organization. The request sparked an hour of work over a simple note because it was going to the "biggest, most important people in the company."

The most important point is that position power exists. Use it to provide vision, mission, and direction. But, don't use position power to strike fear in the hearts and minds of employees. Every employee is equal in an organization; each person just has a different job and a different contribution to make. Treat every employee as your equal.

What do employees want from work? There are five factors that must be present in your workplace for your employees to be happy and motivated at work. Your employees need respect, to be members of the in-crowd, to impact decision making about their jobs, to have the opportunity to grow and develop, and access to reasonable leadership. The following describe what employees want from work:

- Respect is the fundamental right of every employee in every workplace. If people feel as if they are treated with respect, they usually respond with respect and dignified actions. Part of respect is praise and feedback so people know how they are doing at work.

- Employees want to feel as if they are members of the in-crowd. This means that they know and have access to information as quickly as anyone else in your workplace.

- Employees want to learn new skills, develop their capabilities, and grow their knowledge and careers. Making developmental opportunities available to each employee demonstrates your commitment to helping them develop their careers. They appreciate this.

- Employees want to have an impact on decisions that are made about their jobs. Employee involvement and employee empowerment help to create engaged employees willing to put forth their discretionary energy for the business.

- Employees do want leadership. They want a sense of being on the right track, going somewhere that has been defined and is important. They like being part of something bigger than themselves. Employees like to know that someone who is trustworthy, is in charge.

If these five factors existed in every workplace, productivity, motivation, and happiness would soar.

People are the most important resource of your business. Often stated, but seldom totally believed, organizations will learn this important fact going forward, if they haven't already. One of your biggest challenges of this decade will be attracting and retaining a superior workforce. Your Human Resources staff members are key players in recruiting and retaining staff. Your HR staff members should also lead your efforts in training and organization development. They are the heart of helping you form a positive, employee and customer-oriented culture.

With so much responsibility, and so much potential impact on your business, HR should report to the CEO or President of your company. This enables the HR person to speak directly to the person who most closely molds your corporate culture, the President or CEO. This direct contact, without having to work through layers of other managers who may or may not put forth the HR point of view, is important for your business success.

Especially when HR reports to accounting or administration, you are not creating a needed check and balance in your organization. People needs vs. finance needs is a tough balancing act at best. When both are represented by the head of finance, you assure you won't hear both points of view.

Strategically, your head HR person should participate in executive meetings and share decision making for the corporation. This enables the HR group to better understand and participate in managing the business. With thorough knowledge of the business, better decisions and recommendations come from HR. Your recruiting, retention, training, organization development, and culture are recommended and formed from a thorough understanding of your business needs.

Conversely, decisions about the business are made with full understanding about their impact on people, the culture, and the work environment. You enable your HR staff to affect your strategic outcomes. And, this is a positive factor in your business success.

Human Resources leaders need degrees. If you are considering a career in Human Resources, or trying to advance your current career, a Bachelors degree, and even a Masters degree, will assist you to achieve your goals and dreams. Degrees have become more important in most fields, but nowhere has the shift occurred quite as dramatically as in HR. As organizational expectations of the potential contributions of an HR pro have increased, the need for the HR leader to possess both experience and a degree has increased, too. In fact, a degree is becoming essential.

I can't say that I would never consider a candidate for a role in HR leadership who didn't have a degree—never say never—but, why would an organization select a candidate who has experience and no degree, over a candidate with experience and a degree? (I am making the assumption that the organization likes both candidates and their cultural fit and experience are equal.

What I have experienced in hiring, I have found college degrees that have emphasized well-rounded understanding of the fundamentals, quite predictive of future success. We can all name an exception. My father's youngest brother quit school after seventh grade, founded a car spare parts garage in Vai Town, Monrovia, and is now the richest person I know in his town. But he is an exception.

Hiring Human Resources Leaders, Who Have Earned a Degree, Sends a Powerful Message

A degreed HR leader will generally prove more effective and more sought after than a person without a degree. Here's why.

- The staff members the HR leader will supervise increasingly have degrees. An MBA and a Business degree with a concentration in HR or organization development are becoming more common. So are candidates with degrees in psychology, sociology, and other areas of liberal arts. Degreed staff will look up to an HR leader with degrees.

- The staff members whom the HR leader advises will increasingly have degrees. As the HR leader progresses up the organization chart, his or her peers will increasingly have degrees and MBAs. Especially as a company grows and hires more professional staff, degrees become the norm. The HR leader needs to possess the same ticket to be a sought after confidant and advisor. The degree is step one in joining the club.

- Especially for salaried positions, degrees plus experience rank highly among the traits, skills, and characteristics identified as needed and desired from people selected to fill most of the leadership positions in organizations.

- A college degree and the coursework associated with earning that degree have long been touted as producers of well-rounded knowledgeable candidates who can think and solve problems, and who have proven they can stick with a goal and complete it. Just one college website advertises its graduates:

Among Cuttington University graduates, you'll find young men and women prepared to both think critically, and to apply skills practically and professionally in a variety of settings...Cuttington's distinctive integration of the traditional liberal arts with preparation for professions, careers, and community leadership equips our students exceptionally well for excellence in today's increasingly complex world.

The HR leader is usually the education and development leader for the organization. The individual who leads in this role should be able to demonstrate the value of education in their own life.

The HR leader generally serves as the initiator of processes that identify and encourage high potential staff. This role includes encouraging employees to attend school to further develop their skills and capacities. Additionally, the HR leader assesses the need for and often delivers training and development sessions to others in the organization. The degree brings credibility to his or her ability to do these activities.

Recognize that this is an option, and I am unaware of data that support this opinion, but I generally find that HR people without degrees lack knowledge and experience in organization development, strategic business management, and management development. They lack some of the educational and developmental leadership background and skills of their more educated counterparts. At the same time, they often have deeper knowledge in transactional areas as they generally worked their way up over the years from an early payroll or administration job. Indeed, they usually have in-depth knowledge of employment law and policy and procedure making, too.

In summary, a degree is becoming essential for an HR professional who plan a leadership role in an organization. In fact, I believe that a Masters Degree, or even PhD. Will eventually be the degrees of choice for HR leaders. Certification through the society for Human Resources Management is becoming more common as well. Will you be ready to compete for the best HR jobs and opportunities?

Six Disciplines contracted with market research firm, Research for Action, to survey 314 businesses that employ 10-100 people to determine the factors that were most important in their success, some years ago. They found five factors that stood out as most significant. In fact, they found that "high performing organizations scored at least 100% better on these five factors than their competitors." These were the top five success factors:

- The strength of the senior leadership team.
- The organization's ability to attract and retain quality people.
- The organization's ability to adopt a disciplined approach to the business including working "on" the business to create plans and align the employees to execute the business plans.
- High performing companies made strategic use of technology.
- High performing companies developed relationships with trusted outside providers such as attorneys, finance and accounting professionals, and insurance professionals.

These are the big five when successful change management is achieved.

- Effective communication,
- Full and active executive support,
- Employee involvement,
- Organizational planning and analysis and
- Widespread perceived need for the change.

Implementing your change in an organizational environment that is already employee-oriented, with a high level of trust, is a huge plus.

A new manager asked me recently in Perth Amboy, New Jersey how she should go about getting her staff to "buy into" some changes she wants to make in the operation of their department. I asked her whether she wanted to spend the time on the front end necessary for earning staff commitment to the changes. Alternatively, I told her that she could spend her time policing the changes on the back end. Indeed, if staff members reacted too unfavorably, she might even have her ideas sabotaged and/or an open position or two to fill. At the minimum, her staff would experience a lack of motivation and feelings of disgruntlement.

She chose the first path, but not all managers do. You need to recognize that if you want wholehearted commitment to any change, you must involve staff members. The employees who will be expected to implement the change must be involved in the creation of the change. That doesn't mean they set the goal, but they must be significantly involved in the definition and the details.

If you want to foster employee commitment to change, the employee must be involved in designing the changes, implementing the changes, and evaluating the effectiveness of the changes. Employees will never whole- heartedly support a change they were not involved in creating.

Listen with your full attention directed toward understanding what your coworker or staff member needs from you. Many managers, especially, are so used to helping people solve problems that their first course of action is to begin brainstorming solutions and giving advice. Maybe the employee just needs a listening ear. Your best approach is to listen deeply, ask questions for clarification to make sure you understand the situation and then, only then, ask the person what they would like for you. Trust me. They usually know, and often, they breathe a sigh of relief and say, "Thanks for listening."

I have never worked with a client organization in which employees were completely happy with communication. It is one of the toughest issues in organizations. Effective communication requires four components interworking perfectly for "shared meaning," my favorite definition of communication.

- The individual sending the message must present the message clearly and in detail, and radiate integrity and authenticity.
- The person receiving the message must decide to listen, ask questions for clarity, and trust the presenter.

- The delivery method chosen must suit the circumstances and the needs of both the sender and the receiver.

- The content of the message has to resonate and connect, on some level, with the already-held beliefs of the receiver.

With all of this going on in a communication, I think it's a wonder that organizations ever do it well.

An incident occurred recently that made me revisit the subject of disciplinary action, specifically, progressive discipline. I revised the discipline form that the supervisors have long disliked. I think the new one is straight forward and addresses employee actions in behavioral terms.

Telling an employee, "You have a bad attitude," gives the employee no information about the behavior you want to see the employee change or improve. Better? Say, "When you slam your parts down hard on your work bench, you risk breaking the part; you are also disturbing your coworkers. The noise disturbs them and they are concerned about parts flying through the air." Just as you are as specific as possible when you praise or recognize positive employee behavior and contributions, you are specific when you ask an employee to stop or improve negative actions.

I'll bet you'd like to know the incident that precipitated my rewrite of the disciplinary action form. Two employees (who are dating outside of work) held a screaming match in the middle of the plant in view and hearing of most other employees. Check "conduct" for this spectacle. Take a look at the new progressive disciplinary action form (see Appendices). I also added employee counseling steps to make sure the most important aspect of disciplinary action occurs.

Each of us is a radar machine constantly scoping out our environment. Human beings are sensitive to body language, facial expression, posture, movement, tone of voice and more. To effectively communicate, these interpersonal communication dynamics must match your words. Words are distantly useful for people who are scoping out the meaning of a communication.

Without awareness of the whole person, who is doing the communicating, including the factors in interpersonal communication dynamics, you miss much of what is being communicated. At the same time, if you communicate without understanding all of the interpersonal communication dynamics your listener sees and hears, you fail to use powerful aspects of communication.

Your body language, facial expression, posture, movement, and tone of voice can help you emphasize the truth, sincerity, and reliability of your communication. They can also undermine your communication if the words you use are incongruent with the message sent via the interpersonal communication dynamics.

Since communication is shared meaning, your words must send the same message as the other interpersonal communication dynamics. A consistent message ensures effective communication.

If you manage people, work in Human Resources, or care about your friends at work, chances are good that one day you will need to hold a difficult conversation.

People dress inappropriately and unprofessionally for work. Personal hygiene is sometimes unacceptable. Flirtatious behavior can lead to a sexual harassment problem. A messy desk is not a sign of an organized mind. Unreturned pop cans do draw ants.

Vulgar language is professional. Revealing cleavage belongs in a club, a party, or on the beach. Leaving dirty dishes for others to wash is rude.

Have you encountered any of these examples? They're just samples of the types of behavior that cry out for responsible feedback. These steps will help you hold difficult conversations when people need professional feedback.

Steps to Provide Feedback in a difficult Conversation

- Seek permission to provide the feedback. Even if you are the employee's boss, start by stating you have some feedback you'd like to share. Ask if it's a good time or if the employee would prefer to select another time and place. (Within reason, of course.)

- Use a soft entry. Don't drive right into the feedback—give the person a chance to brace for potentially embarrassing feedback. Tell the employee that you need to provide feedback that is difficult to share. If you're uncomfortable with your role in the conversation, you might say that, too. Most people are as uncomfortable providing feedback about an individual's personal dress or habits, as the person receiving the feedback.

- Often, you are in the feedback role because other employees have complained to you about the habit, behavior, or dress. Do not give in to the temptation to amplify the feedback, or excuse your responsibility for the feedback, by stating that a number of coworkers have complained. This heightens the embarrassment and harms the recovery of the person receiving feedback.

- The best feedback is straightforward and simple. Don't beat around the bush. I am talking with you because this is an issue that you need to address for success in this organization.

- Tell the person the impact that changing his or her behavior will have from a positive perspective. Tell the employee how choosing to do nothing will affect their career and job.

- Reach agreement about what the individual will do to change their behavior. Set a due date—tomorrow, in some cases. Set a time frame to review progress in others.

- Follow-up. The fact that the problem exists means that backsliding is possible; further clarification may also be necessary. Then, more feedback and possibly, disciplinary action are possible next steps.

You can become effective at holding difficult conversations. Practice and these steps will help build your comfort level to hold difficult conversations. After all, a difficult conversation can make the difference between success and failure for a valued employee. Care enough to hold the difficult conversation.

Have you ever worked alongside an employee who had poor personal hygiene, foul smelling clothes or breath, or an annoying personal habit like making clicking noises? Or worse, the employee drinks heavily in the evening and then exudes the smell f alcohol, often mixed with the equally fetid smell of coffee and cigarettes, all day at work?

Or, worst on the list of most challenging issues, the employee's breath and pores exude a spicy aroma that makes you ill; the employee's clothes are clean, but he or she appears to bathe infrequently, and you're positive that saying anything would be culturally insensitive. Welcome to the workplace situations from hell.

Start by reading How to Hold a Difficult Conversation for some initial insight into these challenging discussions. Then, integrate these new tips about holding difficult conversations into your feedback approach.

More Ideas for Holding Difficult Conversations

- Start with a soft approach to set the employee at ease, but don't beat around the bush. The employee's level of anxiety is already sky high and making more small talk while he waits for the bad news to emerge, is cruel. Once you've told him that you want to discuss a difficult topic, move right into the topic of your difficult conversation.

- Tell the employee directly what the problem is as you perceive it. If you talk around the issue or soften the impact of the issue too much, the employee may never get that the problem is serious. If you reference the problem as "some of our employees do the following," the employee may never understand that you mean him.

- Whenever possible, attach the feedback to a business issue. This is not a personal vendetta; the difficult conversation has a direct business purpose. Perhaps other employees don't want to participate on his team, and you've noticed the lack of volunteers. Perhaps his appearance is affecting the perception of customers about the quality of the organization's products. Maybe, an irritating mannerism has caused a customer to request a different sales rep. Make the business purpose of the conversation clear.

- You also need to let the employee know that not only is the behavior affecting the business and the employee's coworkers, but it is also affecting the employee's career. Express directly the impact you believe the behavior is having on the employee's potential promotions, raises, career opportunities, and relationships in the workplace.

- I receive frequent emails asking me if a training solution is appropriate in these instances. The managers who write suggest that they will provide a grooming and professionalism seminar for all employees to attend. The employee with the problem will get the message via the training. It isn't going to happen. The employee with the problem will not get that you mean him and you will have subjected countless others to training they didn't need.

I am not opposed to professionalism training, dress code training, and similar activities. I have even sponsored a fashion show to demonstrate appropriate business casual dress.

I am opposed to training as a means to correct the personal problems of individuals. The worst suggestion that I have seen recently? Train just the individuals who are perceived by organization members to have the problem. This is offensive and discriminatory. Address the issue with the employee—individually.

- Be sensitive to the fact that different cultures have different norms and standards for appearance, bathing, and dress. I'd probably leave this discussion to the employee's manager, but your workplace is justified in asking employees to embrace the cultural standards of the workplace in which the employee is working. This is especially true if nonconformance to the standard is interfering with the harmony and productivity of your workplace.

- Be sensitive to the difference in cooking and eating traditions, too. A woman confided to me recently that her fellow students had laughed at her and made fun of her because she always smelled like curry and garlic and other pungent spices. As a working adult, she has toned down the amount of spice in her cooking, but she was injured by the thoughtlessness for years. Heck, my own father used to regularly complain that I smelled like garlic, and he didn't mean it as a compliment; he was not fond of garlic, and I am.

- If an employee has repeatedly tried to correct a hygiene issue such as bad breath, and is not making progress, suggest that the employee see a physician to determine if an underlying medical condition might be causing the problem. Your thoughtfulness could save an employee's life.

- Finally, if you are the employee's supervisor, you owe it to the employee to hold the difficult conversation. Especially, if other employees have complained to you, understand that if you don't hold the difficult conversation, the employee's coworkers will.

And, they may not hold the conversation effectively with the goal of minimizing embarrassment and discomfort. A bottle of deodorant might show up on the employee's desk. Soap has been placed in employee mailboxes, in my client companies. Nasty notes have also been left in mailboxes and on chairs. None of these actions contribute to a harmonious workplace. Furthermore, the employee can justifiably charge the employer with allowing harassment and a hostile work environment.

Care enough about the employee and your productive, harmonious workplace to hold the difficult conversation.

If you manage people, work in Human Resources, or care about your friends at work, chances are good that one day you will need to hold a difficult conversation.

People dress inappropriately and unprofessionally for work. Personal hygiene is sometimes unacceptable. Flirtatious behavior can lead to a sexual harassment problem. A messy desk is not a sign of an organized mind. Unreturned pop cans do draw ants.

Vulgar language is unprofessional. Revealing cleavage belongs in a club, a party, or on the beach. Leaving dirty dishes for others to wash is rude.

Have you encountered any of these examples? They're just samples of the types of behavior that cry out for responsible feedback. These steps will help you hold difficult conversations when people need professional feedback.

Steps to Provide Feedback in a Difficult Conversation

- Seek permission to provide the feedback. Even if you are the employee's boss, start by stating you have some feedback you'd like to share. Ask if it's a good time or if the employee would prefer to select another time and place. (Within reason, of course.)

- Use a soft entry. Don't dive right into the feedback—give the person a chance to brace for potentially embarrassing feedback. Tell the employee that you need to provide feedback that is difficult to share. If you're uncomfortable with your role in the conversation, you might say that, too. Most people are as uncomfortable providing feedback about an individual's personal dress or habits, as the person receiving the feedback.

- Often, you are in the feedback role because other employees have complained to you about the habit, behavior, or dress. Do not give in to the temptation to amplify the feedback, or excuse your responsibility for the feedback, by stating that a number of coworkers have complained. This heightens the embarrassment and harms the recovery of the person receiving feedback.

- The best feedback is straightforward and simple. Don't beat around the bush. I am talking with you because this is an issue that you need to address for success in this organization.

- Tell the person the impact that changing his or her behavior will have from a positive perspective. Tell the employee how choosing to do nothing will affect their career and job.

- Reach agreement about what the individual will do to change their behavior. Set a due date—tomorrow, in some cases. Set a time frame to review progress in others.

- Follow-up. The fact that the problem exists means that backsliding is possible; further clarification may also be necessary. Then, more feedback and possibly disciplinary action are possible next steps.

You can become effective at holding difficult conversations. Practice and these steps will help build your comfort level to hold difficult conversations. After all, a difficult conversation can make the difference between success and failure for a valued employee. Care enough to hold the difficult conversation.

Have you ever worked alongside an employee who had poor personal hygiene, foul smelling clothes or breath, or an annoying personal habit like making clicking noises? Or worse, the employee drinks heavily in the evening and then exudes the smell of alcohol, often mixed with the equally fetid smell of coffee and cigarettes, all day awork?

Or, worst on the list of most challenging issues, the employee's breath and pores exude a spicy aroma that makes you ill; the employee's clothes are clean, but he or she appears to bathe infrequently, and you're positive that saying anything would be culturally insensitive.

Actions for Leading and Directing an HR Office

A recent survey at a client company gave the company high marks for communication and teamwork. The lowest score was in shared vision, mission, and direction. Staff felt they understood their team goals well, but did not understand, and thus could not support, the overall company direction. The lack of shared vision and mission scared people. The company downsized this fall and had experienced some bumpy months. Fear that no one knew where the company was going was the scariest of all to staff members. These fears were allayed by company leaders providing more information and meeting more frequently with staff. During times of change: changing direction, changing business models and more, the power of leader communication of a clear mission and vision for the future cannot be underestimated.

During an interview with a manager, she criticized her boss for not leading. She said that, when a decision was needed, her boss immediately went to the group for consensus rather than providing the direction the group needed. In another organization, the CEO (leader) often lamented that he repeatedly told people where to head and they didn't go there. He always wondered why they didn't do what he told them to do, despite the fact that he was not doing it. The secret in both of these cases is simple, but profound. The leader needs to lead the pack, not stand back and follow where the group decides to go. The leader leads. Many leaders wait for that consensus and fail to provide direction. Others fail to move in the appropriate direction while expecting and telling others to do so. Neither works.

Leaders of organizations, especially people with high level titles and ownership positions, establish and maintain the level of comfort that other employees experience when they are asked to speak up. In most organizations, the willingness of employees, even managers, to speak up in disagreement with the higher level person is appallingly bad. Why is this so? Is it because people lack personal and professional courage at work? Or, are they too beholden to these executives for their job?

In any case, it is the leader who establishes the tone and the work environment in which people choose—or choose not—to exercise personal courage and freedom of expression. If the leader has traditionally proved to be genuinely open to comments and criticism, people are willing to agree, disagree, and express opinions. If the leader has not been open to disagreement or debate, his or her actions speak loudly and clearly to staff. And, unfortunately, it only takes one exhibition of closed mindedness, or worse, punishing the speaker, for staff to learn whether their opinions are actually wanted.

The good leader, who wants to take advantage of the experience, knowledge, and thoughtfulness of talented staff, remembers this. The good leader is aware of their power to encourage of stifle opinions and debate. They use this power to genuinely appreciate and encourage input, debate, and differing opinions.

When using temporary staff, do not feel that you are compelled to hire them just because they've worked for you for ninety days or more. In fact, examine the success of a temp at thirty days. If you are not certain that he will make a superior employee, replace him with another temp. Your supervisors tend to "settle" for "good enough" because the temp comes to work every day and does the job. The supervisor will not have to constantly train new temps and this is appreciated. It is not, however, the way to obtain a superior staff. I tell supervisors they may hire the top five percent of their temporary staff members—only the very best.

Many people are thrilled when they find a qualified candidate for an open position. I'm not. I like to find two or more candidates so managers have a choice. The process of deciding among several candidates helps people clarify what they really want from the new employee. It enables them to review candidate qualifications and experience so there are no surprises after the hire. The decision process helps employees "own" the candidate so he or she is welcomed into the organization. The process keeps managers from experiencing selection regret in which they think the best candidate was just another advertisement or resume away. Ideally, when you select your new employee, you select from two or three qualified candidates to get the best fit for your culture and needed skills and experience.

A salary negotiation window exists from the time you offer a job to a candidate until the acceptable of the job by your selected candidate. The results of this negotiation can leave a candidate feeling wanted or devalued. The results of this negotiation can leave the employer excited to welcome the candidate or feeling as if he lost. A positive employer and a positive employee are the result of a successful salary negotiation.

My last salary negotiation failed—and I couldn't figure out why until I received feedback from a friend of the candidate later. Hiring a mid to low level business development staff member, we offered the candidate a certain sum of compensation (in the 40s) with bonus potential into the fifties. Both the hiring manager and I provided her with the same information about what we planned to pay our selected candidate. She indicated that our projected salary met her needs. But, when I offered her the position, she countered with a request for a higher pay than the negotiated one. Since we were already at the top of our range, we declined to counter. Only later did I discover that a third person had told her fifties when she asked about the salary, meaning salary plus bonus. In her wishful thinking, she ignored the hiring manager and myself, and added more to the offer she expected.

So, we all lost, but especially our candidate lost as we had offered her the job of her dreams at the company of her dreams.

The most important learning is, of course, that only one person should be designated to discuss and negotiate salary with a candidate. Others can contribute in the background, but negotiations should be conducted by one person, usually a human resources staff person.

People forget that the purpose of a job interview is not just to get the job. Sound strange to you? It's not. You go to a job interview to discover whether your talents, abilities, interests and direction are a good fit for the job, the company, and the company's mission.

During a job interview, you have the chance to present yourself professionally. Sometimes, if all else is a good match, you are selected for the job. Sometimes, the company's needs and your strengths are not a good match. The job interview is the right time to discover this.

Smart Candidates Turn Down Second Job Interviews

Being exactly who you are—your best professional self—during a job interview is critical. Let your personality, interests and abilities shine through during the job interview. Provide the information needed for the employer to find out that you are a great match for the job—if you really are. Recently, two candidates turned down the opportunity to participate in a second job interview with a client company. Rather than feeling badly about it—they were both excellent candidates—I called each of them to discover why they had turned down a second job interview. (A candidate who turns down a second job interview is rare indeed, and I wanted to know why.)

The first candidate, who currently works in advertising, said that she had participated in interviews at several companies. After learning about the job of an HR Assistant, she decided to pursue a different position within business for her work. She has eliminated both advertising and human resources as current career choices.

The second candidate, after learning about the benefits and career paths available in a smaller company, decided to stay with her major-sized employer. Sadly, locking on golden handcuffs at age twenty-five, and despite the fact that her career interests were more congruent with the smaller company, she eschewed the opportunity to certain her benefits and stay in her little box on the big organization chart.

Both candidates made good choices within their current understanding of themselves. The company is pleased that the managers did not invest months of work in training only to have the employee leave for a different opportunity. The employer was also happy he will not need to start over again in an employee search any time soon. (The company found the "right" employee during the next interview.)

This is an example of the interview process working well for both the candidate and for the company. When the appropriate match between talents, interests, direction, and abilities is missing, both the company and the candidate need to run—don't walk—to their next interview.

Reference Checking

Reference checking is often relegated to Human Resources in organizations. In my mind, that's not who should own reference checking. The manager of the position should check the employment references. He or she has the most to lose if the needed skills and cultural fit don't work out. The manager's "feel" for the viability of the candidate is also key for the person's eventual success as an employee.

Sure, Human Resources can:

- Own the reference checking process,
- Check references for entry level jobs, and
- Check the candidate's list of prepped references.

But for most jobs, the manager of the position is the best person to reference check. This is especially true for talking with past employers and the candidate's former bosses. The manager knows the technical qualifications a candidate must bring to a position. The manager knows the appropriate questions to ask the current and/or former employer about the candidate's work. The manager can listen for statements that indicate cultural fit and that the strengths listed match the strengths you need.

Before you turn your managers loose of reference checking, however, training in how to check references is required. Since you never get a second chance, particularly with the candidate's former manager, doing it right the first time is paramount. And, this training needs to include how to reach the manager, how to bypass the HR office, if possible, and how to help the reference open up and communicate about the potential employee. Here's a handy reference checking format that you can modify for use in your organization.

How to Manage Gossip on the Jobsite

Gossip is rampant in most workplaces. Sometimes, it seems as if people have nothing better to do than gossip about each other. They gossip about the company, their coworkers, and their managers. They frequently take a partial truth and turn it into a whole speculative truth. Many employees gossip about the amount of money they make—and often, they don't tell the truth. So, unhappy coworkers beat a path to the HR door asking about their own salary.

Except a certain amount of gossip; people want to know what is going on in their workplace, and they like to discuss work issues. The key is to know when the gossip is out-of-hand. You need to act if the gossip is:

- Disrupting the workplace and the business of work,
- Hurting employees' feelings,
- Damaging interpersonal relationships, or
- Injuring employee motivation and morale.

If you find yourself having to address gossip frequently, you may want to examine your workplace to understand the consistent themes in the gossip. Consider that you may not be sharing enough information with employees. It is also possible that employees don't trust you and are afraid to ask about important topics. If gossip has been unmanaged in the past, gossip tends to become a negative aspect of your work culture. So, don't let negative gossip go unaddressed.

You can manage gossip exactly as you would manage any other negative behavior from an employee in your workplace. Use a coaching approach, when possible, to help the employee improve his or her behavior. But, when needed, gossip management starts with a serious talk between the employee and the manager or supervisor. If the discussion of the negative impacts of the employee's gossip has no effect on subsequent behavior, begin the process of progressive discipline with a verbal warning, then a formal written verbal warning for the employee's personnel file.

If you assertively deal with gossip, you will create a work culture and environment that does not support gossip.

Think you don't gossip? Take this quiz to find out…

1. You and your friends are at a party. You see one of your friends smoking marijuana. You:

2. Pray for him.

3. Add him to your youth group prayer list.

4. Tell everyone at school.

5. Tell a parent and pray for your friend.

6. You walk by the magazine counter and see a headline about your favorite actress cheating on her boyfriend. You:

7. Check your wallet. You must know the details!

8. You're tempted, but you walk away.

9. Leave the magazine, but check out the story online. You won't financially support those types of magazines.

10. You walk away. Those magazines are junk.

11. You overhear your friend's boyfriend telling everyone lies about their date on Saturday. You:

12. Confront him right there and tell him to take back the lies.

13. Run and tell your friend.

14. Post the story on MySpace.

15. Spread lies about him. Let's see how he feels!

16. Your friends are sitting around when one starts telling you what she heard one girl did at the party last weekend. You:

17. Listen intently. Then call everyone you know. You can't keep a story that good quiet!

18. Listen and analyze her actions with your friends.

19. Go get another drink while they finish talking about it.

20. Tell them you don't feel comfortable talking about it and change the subject.

21. You and your friends usually talk about:

22. A. Dating, friends, people at school

23. What's going on in your lives.

24. Sports, school, movies, music.

25. Teachers.

26. Your friend confides in you that she's pregnant. You:

27. Tell everyone.

28. Tell your parents, because you need to know how to deal with it.

29. Write about it in your School Journal.

30. Tell no one. Just pray to God what to do.

31. How many times a week do you hear yourself saying, "Did you hear about….?"

32. At least once a day

33. 2 to 5

34. 1 to 2

35. Never.

Scoring Key

1. A = 4, B = 2, C = 1, D = 3

2. A = 1, B = 3, C = 2, D = 4

3. A = 4, B = 3, C = 2, D = 1

4. A = 1, B = 2, C = 3, D = 4

5. A = 1, B = 3, C = 4, D = 2

6. A = 1, B = 3, C = 2, D = 4

7. A = 1, B = 2, C = 3, D = 4

Your Scores:

1 to 14—*The Gossip.* You are a gossip. You thrive on gossip and spreading news about others. Yet watch out, because people are probably gossiping about you, too. If you are trying to be a good Christian, you may want to look closer at what the Bible is telling you about your gossip behavior and learn to stop our gossiping in its tracks.

15 to 21—*Wishy-Wash.* You don't gossip all the time, but it may be something you want to work on. You may like to hear gossip more than you spread it. Maybe you like to read gossip magazines. Still, you may want to work on walking away from gossip as it starts so that you can be a better witness to those around you.

22 to 28—*The Anti-Gossip.* You are the anti-gossip. You tend to see gossip for what it is and confront it. You know that what you say reflects on the Lord, and; you try to be more encouraging. You have a good understanding of what the Bible tells you about gossip, and you try to live the Word in your life.

Were you surprised by your results? If so, you may want to read more about gossip's effects and what the Bible has to say about gossip so that you can start being a better witness to those around you.

How to Manage an Exhausted Employee

An exhausted employee is an employer's nightmare. You know the occasional employee I am talking about. He doesn't show up for work, calls in sick, and milks the time off policy, always walking on the edge, but never falling off. He walks the edge of the work policies and processes, too.

He does just enough to stay employed but doesn't grow professionally nor contribute like your other employees. He sometimes reaches his goals but exhibits a general lack of enthusiasm. The hallmark of the exhausted employee is that he is always walking on the edge between succeeding and failing.

Some exhausted employees actively criticize the company and its policies, not through suggested routes, but in e-mail, at the water cooler, and in the employee lunchroom, Palm wine booths or even in checker playing centers around town. Others are constantly unhappy with whatever policy or direction the company sets. Their unhappiness runs all over their coworkers as they complain, gossip, and criticize. Whatever form of behavior your exhausted employee exhibits, it won't go away without your intervent5ion. Bad habits, like good habits, become ingrained in workplace behavior.

The Impact of the Exhausted Employee

The exhausted employee impacts your workplace and employees negatively, constantly, and insidiously. Smart employees shun the exhausted employee, realizing the impact he has on their positive workplace morale and productivity. But employees who feel a bit like he does about a change, the workplace in general, or their jobs, are quick to echo the exhausted employee's point of view. This further poisons your workplace morale and productivity.

If you let the exhausted employee get away with this behavior, you train him or her that the behavior is acceptable. The person's coworkers, who are probably picking up the slack, become demoralized because they work hard and contribute and see that the exhausted employee does not. Additionally, they lose respect for your management, and possibly their faith in the company, because you fail to deal with a problem that everyone in your workplace sees.

Your Responsibilities to Deal with the Exhausted Employee

The exhausted employee's coworkers depend on you to deal with the problem. They may make cutting remarks, shun the non-performer, or talk quietly among themselves, but they don't feel enabled or equipped to deal with the borderline performer. They just feel his impact on their work and workplace. And, they're right.

Coworkers can do their little bits to encourage the exhausted employee to contribute. They can make norms for their team, give coworker feedback, and express unhappiness, but the exhausted employee has no obligation to change or improve. The behavior of the exhausted employee is ultimately the manager's responsibility to address.

How to Approach the exhausted Employee

Your first step with an exhausted employee is to figure out what went wrong. Something did go wrong. This will give you insight into what caused the behavior that is troubling your workplace. Most employees start out enthusiastic and excited about their new job. They find their enthusiasm punctured somewhere along the way. Or, they puncture their own enthusiasm; it works both ways in the workplace. Figuring out what happened is key if you are committed to help the exhausted employee become, not an exhausted employee, but a contributing member of your work community.

It's a rare employee who wakes up in the morning and decides to have a miserable day at work. It's a rare employee who wants to feel failure as he leaves the workplace daily. Yes, a rare employee, but they do exist and I guarantee, the employee believes it's not his fault, it's yours. You are the problem or his workplace is the problem.

Once you've worked with the employee to discover the source of his unhappiness and low morale, you can assist the employee to do something about it. With an exhausted employee, this is the tough step. First, he has to own the responsibility for his subsequent actions and reactions to workplace happenings that may have occurred years ago.

This is a tough step for you, too. You may decide his concerns and unhappiness are legitimate. If so, a sincere apology is in order, even if you had nothing to do with the occurrences that that generated the problem. At the very least, an acknowledgement that you believe that some of his low morale is legitimate may be in order. It also makes sense to ask what about the work system is causing the employee to fail.

You may also decide he brought his lousy attitude to your workplace and your company did an inadequate job of screening out a potentially poorly performing employee. Regardless of the details, on some level, the employee must own that his reaction to the circumstances belongs to him. He must own his chosen reaction. Indeed, our reactions to the changing circumstances around us may be the only factor that is always under our control in most situations.

Next Steps in Dealing With the Exhausted Employee

Whatever you decide about why your exhausted employee is an exhausted employee, these are actions you can try.

- Help the exhausted employee see what's in it for him to succeed and improve. Both personal and professional gains result from improved performance and a commitment to succeed.

- Assure the employee that you have faith in her ability to succeed. Sometimes supportive words from a supervisor or manager are the first she's received in years.

- Help the employee set several short-term, achievable goals. These should be time based and have clear outcomes about which you agree. Some of these goals can address employee "attitude" in behavioral terms. By this I mean that it is not possible for you and the employee to share a clear picture of "bad attitude." But, you can share a picture about the behaviors the employee exhibits that make you think "bad attitude." Then, monitor progress.

- Make sure the employee has something to do that he likes every day.

CONFLICT RESOLUTION

How to Encourage a Meaningful Work Conflict

Organization leaders are responsible for creating a work environment that enables people to thrive. If turf wars, disagreements and differences of opinion escalate into interpersonal conflict, you must intervene immediately. Not intervening is not an option if you value your organization and your positive culture. In conflict-ridden situations, your mediation skill and interventions are critical.

Actions to Avoid in Conflict Resolution

Do not avoid the conflict, hoping it will go away. Trust me. It won't. Even if the conflict appears to have been superficially put to rest, it will rear its ugly head whenever stress increases or a new disagreement occurs. An unresolved conflict or interpersonal disagreement festers just under the surface in your work environment. It burbles to the surface whenever enabled, and always at the worst possible moment. This, too, shall pass, is not an option—ever.

Do not meet separately with people in conflict. If you allow each individual to tell their story to you, you risk polarizing their positions. The person in conflict has a vested interest in making himself or herself "right" if you place yourself in the position of judge and jury. The sole goal of the employee, in this situation, is to convince you of the merits of their case.

Do not believe, for even a moment, the only people who are affected by the conflict are the participants. Everyone in your office and every employee, with whom the conflicting employees interact, is affected by the stress. People feel as if they are walking on eggshells in the presence of the antagonists. This contributes to the creation of a hostile work environment for other employees. In worst case scenarios, your organization members take sides and your organization is divided. Conflict avoidance is most frequently the topic when conflict in organizations is discussed. Conflict resolution—as quickly as possible—is the second most frequent topic. This is bad news because meaningful work conflict is a cornerstone in health, successful organizations. Conflict is necessary for effective problem solving and for effective interpersonal relationships.

These statements may seem unusual to you. If you are like many people, you avoid conflict in your daily work life. You see only the negative results of conflict. Especially in the Human Resources profession, or as a manager or supervisor, you may even find that you spend too much of your precious time mediating disputes between coworkers.

Why People don't participate in appropriate Work Conflict

There are many reasons why people don't stand up for their beliefs and bring important differences to the table. (In organizations, this translates into people nodding in unison when the manager asks if the group agrees, but then complaining about the decision later.) Conflict is usually uncomfortable. Many people don't know how to participate in and manage work conflict in a positive way. In a poorly carried out conflict, people sometimes get hurt. They become defensive because they feel under attack personally. People have to work with certain people every single day, so they are afraid conflict will harm these necessary ongoing relationships.

Why Appropriate Work Conflict is Important

Effectively managed work conflict has many positive results for your organization, however. When people can disagree with each other and lobby for different ideas, your organization is healthier. Disagreements often result in a more thorough study of options and better decisions and direction. According to Peter Block, in The Empowered Manager: Positive Political Skills at Work, if you are unwilling to participate in organizational politics and conflict, you will never accomplish the things that are important to you at work, your work mission. And, that would be tragic. So, knowing how to raise issues and participate in meaningful work conflict is key to your success in work and in life. These tips will help.

How to Participate in a Health Work Conflict

Create a work environment in which health conflict is encouraged by setting clear expectations. Foster an organizational culture or environment in which differences of option are encouraged. Make differences the expectation and health debate about issues and ideas the norm. Placing emphasis on the common goals people share within your organization can help/ People have a tendency to focus on the differences experienced with other rather than focusing on the beliefs and goals they have in common with each other.

If organizational goals are aligned and all employees are moving in the same direction, healthy work conflict about how to get there is respected. If you are a manager or team leader, do this by asking others to express their opinion before you speak your own. Tell people that you want them to speak up when they disagree or have an opinion that is different from others in the group.

Reward, recognize, and thank people who are willing to take a stand and support their position. You can publicly thank people who are willing to disagree with the direction of a group. Your recognition system, bonus systems, pay and benefits package, and performance management process should all reward the employees who practice personal organizational courage and pursue appropriate work conflict.

These employees speak up to disagree or propose a different approach even in the face of pressure from the group to agree. They lobby passionately for their cause or belief, yet, when all the debating is over, they support the decisions made by the team just as passionately.

If you experience little dissention in your group, examine your own actions. If you believe you want different opinions expressed and want to avoid "group think," and you experience little disagreement from staff, examine your own actions. Do you, non-verbally or verbally, send the message that it is really not okay to disagree? Do you put employees in a "hot seat" when they express an opinion? Do they get "in trouble" if they are wrong or a predicted solution fails to work?

Look inside yourself personally, and even seek feedback from a trusted advisor or staff member, if the behavior of your team tells you that you are inadvertently sending the wrong message.

Expect people to support their opinions and recommendations with data and facts. Divergent opinions are encouraged, but the opinions are arrived at through the study of data and facts. Staff members are encouraged to collect data that will illuminate the process or problem.

Create a group norm that conflict around ideas and direction is expected and that personal attacks are not tolerated. Any group that comes together regularly to lead an organization or department, solve a problem, or to improve or create a process would benefit from group norms. These are the relationship guidelines or rules group members agree to follow. They often include the expectation that all members will speak honestly, that all opinions are equal, and that each person will participate. These guidelines also set up the expectation that personal attacks are not tolerated whereas healthy debate about ideas and options is encouraged.

Provide employees with training in healthy conflict and problem solving skills. Sometimes people fail to stand up for their beliefs because they don't know how to do so comfortably. Your staff will benefit from education and training in interpersonal communication, problem solving, conflict resolution, and particularly, non-defensive communication. Goal setting, meeting management, and leadership will also help employees exercise their freedom of speech.

Look for signs that a conflict about a solution or direction is getting out of hand. Exercise your best observation skills and notice whether tension is becoming unhealthy. Listen for criticism of fellow staff members, an increase in the number and severity of "digs" or putdowns, and negative comments about the solution or process. Are secret meetings increasing?

In one organization that I worked, staff members hold e-mail wars in which the nastiness of the e-mails grows and the list of staff members copied can include the whole organization. If you observe the tension and conflict is endangering your workplace harmony, hold a conflict resolution meeting with the combatants immediately. Yes, you do need to mediate. It's okay to have positive conflict but not to allow negative conflict to destroy your work environment.

Hire people who you believe will add value to your organization with their willingness to problem solve and debate. Behavioral interview questions will help you assess the assertiveness of your potential employees. You want to hire people who are willing to act boldly and who are unconcerned about whether they are well-liked. Look and listen for situations in which the potential employee has stood up for his beliefs, worked with a team to solve problems, or pushed an unpopular agenda at work. Yes, you want a harmonious workplace but not at the sacrifice of everyone's success.

Make executive compensation dependent upon the success of the organization as a whole as well as the accomplishment of individual goals. Pay executives part of their compensation based on the success of the total organization. This ensures that people are committed to the same goals and direction. They will look for the best approach, the best ideas, and the best solution, not just the one that will benefit their won area of interest. This will also ensure that the people in their organizations spend their time problem solving and solution seeking rather than finger-pointing, blaming, and looking to see who is guilty when a problem occurs or a commitment is missed.

If you are using all of the first nine tips, and healthy work conflict is not occurring...You need to sit down with the people who report to you directly and with their direct reporting staff and ask them why. Some positive, problem solving discussion might allow your group to identify and rectify any problem that stands in the way of open, healthy, positive, constructive work conflict and debate. The future success of your organization depends upon your staff's willingness to participate in healthy work conflict, so this discussion is worth your time.

Promotions

The Company seeks to hire or promote the best-qualified individual for open positions. To achieve that goal, the following procedures have been adopted:

The supervisor will review and update the job analysis and job description for the open position and recommend the salary range. If none exist, they will be created in accordance with the policy on job analyses, job descriptions, and compensation.

The Human Resources department will review the material prepared by the supervisor and make any needed corrections in consultation with the supervisor.

The job opening will be posted for current employees and advertised in the media most likely to be read by persons qualified for the job.

Applications for the position will be accepted for at least a 2-week period.

The supervisor and the Human Resources recruiter will review the applications and schedule interviews. Generally, applicants will be interviewed unless their applications show objectively that they are not qualified for the position. For example, if the position requires a person with spelling skills and the application contains misspelled words, the person can be rejected without an interview.

The supervisor, the next level of management, and the recruiter will interview the candidates. Generally, applicants will be interviewed by at least two of the three. Again, if the first interview reveals facts that show the person is not qualified, the person can be rejected after the other two interviewers are consulted and agree. For example, if the position requires a clean and neat appearance and the individual appears for the interview unbathed and in dirty clothes, the person can be rejected.

The interviewers will use the same questions and the same rating sheets. The questions and rating sheets will be based on the job analysis. If necessary, the questions and rating sheets will be updated. If any changes are made, the new questions and rating sheets are to be reviewed by the manager of Equal Employment Opportunity (EEO) compliance.

Once candidates have been interviewed twice, the three interviewers will rank the candidates based on the objectively observed qualities. If there is a clearly preferred candidate, that person will be interviewed by the third individual. If that person's objective evaluation agrees with the previous ranking, an offer will be extended. If there is no clearly preferred candidate, the top five candidates will be interviewed by whichever person has not yet interviewed the candidate. The ranking process will be repeated. If there is still no clearly preferred candidate, the manager of EEO compliance will be consulted to ensure that there is no appearance of unlawful discrimination. If there is no such appearance, the position will be offered to the top-ranked candidate. If it appears there may have been unlawful discrimination, appropriate corrective action will be taken.

The manager of Human Resources and the manager of EEO compliance will monitor the promotion system to ensure that supervisors and recruiters are not unlawfully rejecting candidates.

Leave of Absence
Statement of Policy

It is the policy of the Company to grant a leave of absence (medical, personal, funeral, or military) to regular full-time employees in good standing for reasons acceptable to the Company.

General Provisions

1. An employee anticipating an absence of 5 days or more must apply for a leave of absence. Failure to obtain a leave of absence will be considered as a resignation.

2. All leaves of absence require the approval of two higher levels of management. Medical leaves require the approval of the manager of compensation and benefits.

3. All leaves must have a specific duration and return-to-work date determined at the time the leave is granted. Failure to return to work on the determined return-to-work day will be considered as a resignation by the employee.

4. Group-term life insurance, medical, and dental benefits may be continued during a leave of absence by making the required application. Continuation coverage under COBRA (see COBRA) may also apply. Arrangements must be made with the benefits department prior to the leave. It is the responsibility of the employee and manager to notify the benefits department and to make these arrangements.

5. Sick leave and vacation benefits do not accrue during a leave of absence.

6. Generally, the Company does not guarantee that a person's job will be held while they are on leave of absence. Usually, if available, an employee returning to work on the date the leave/disability ends will be reinstated to his or her previous job status or one of similar salary and responsibilities with no break in service. Normally, if a position is not available, an employee will be placed on preferential hiring status for positions for which he or she is qualified. As always, the most qualified candidate will be selected for open positions. This policy may be varied to accommodate applicable law.

7. Except as noted, compensation will not be paid during leaves.

8. The Company has the right to initiate a leave of absence for any employee when in its sole judgment such a leave is appropriate.

A Company-initiated leave of absence will require prior approval of the respective vice president and executive director of personnel.

Compensation will cease when in the sole judgment of the Company, the employee is available to return to work.

Compensation due under this provision will be reduced by any benefit payments for which the employee is eligible from other sources including, but not limited to, Social Security and unemployment.

Provisions—Personal Leave

1. An employee requesting a personal leave must have worked full time a minimum of 6 continuous months prior to the request.

2. A personal leave of up to 90 days may be granted and may under special circumstances be extended at the discretion of the Company for up to an additional 90 days.

3. Normally, personal leaves of absence are without pay and granted at the discretion of the Company.

4. An employee returning from a personal leave may be reinstated to his or her former position or to one of like status and pay whenever possible. If immediate placement is not possible, the employee will be placed on preferential hire status.

Provisions—Medical Leave

1. The intent of a medical leave of absence is to provide an employee the necessary time to recover from an injury or illness disabling him or her for a period of time exceeding 5 days.

2. An employee is eligible to apply for a medical leave of absence upon completion of 3 months of continuous full-time employment.

3. To request consideration for a medical leave, the employee must complete the Medical Leave Request form and obtain the signatures of the next two higher levels of management. Final approval will come from the manager of compensation and benefits. For the request to be considered, the employee must attach a physician's statement, including prognosis and expected date of return.

4. Medical leaves may be approved for up to 6 months. In no instance will a medical leave be extended beyond 6 months. For disabilities expected to last beyond 6 months, the employee should immediately apply for Social Security, Medicare, or other disability coverage.

5. The Company reserves the right to require an examination by a physician of its choice if there is a question regarding the employee's physical ability to start or remain on a medical leave status.

6. An employee returning to work on the date the disability ends will be reinstated to his or her previous job status if available, or one of similar salary and responsibilities, with no break in service. If a position is not available, an employee will be placed on preferential hiring status for positions for which he or she is qualified, unless otherwise provided by law. As always, the most qualified candidate will be selected for open positions.

7. An employee returning to work after a medical leave must provide his or her immediate supervisor with a written release from a licensed physician to resume expected job duties. This release must be forwarded to personnel and reviewed prior to the employee's return to work.

Note: Salaried employees may be eligible for salary continuance.

Provisions—Funeral Leave

1. An employee must notify the immediate supervisor as soon as possible upon learning of a death in the family.

2. Employees will be allowed up to 3 days' leave if necessary to attend the funeral of a member of the immediate family (spouse, child or stepchild, parent or stepparent, parent-in-law, legal guardian, or grandparent).

- Hourly, nonexempt employees will not receive compensation for the time taken off.

- Salaried (exempt and nonexempt) employees will receive compensation for the time taken off.

Provisions—Military Leave

1. An employee may take time off work to fulfill his or her annual training obligation or if required to report for extended active duty.

2. A regular full-time employee with 1 year of continuous service will be paid the difference between the military allowance and the current base rate for a maximum of 2 weeks in any calendar year for annual training. If an employee decides to use earned vacation time, this will not be supplemented during the same time period with compensation.

3. An employee on active or inactive duty with an armed forces regular or reserve unit will be returned to his or her former position or to one of like status and pay to the extent required by law.

Provisions—Sick Leave

1. Salaried employees are expected to be at work if they are not disabled because of illness or injury. However, in the event of illness or injury, the salaried employee with a minimum of 3 months' service will be compensated for days away from work not to exceed 5 working days a year.

2. Sick days are not cumulative from year to year. Hourly employees are not eligible for sick leave.

3. All sick leave and short-term disability is recorded on an Absence Report form.

Procedures

1. A request for a leave of absence must be made on the Absence Report form, having the approval of the next two higher levels of management.

- The date the leave starts and the expected return date must be established and documented on the Absence Report form.

- The Absence Report form must be filed in the employee's personnel file.

- The human resources department is responsible for controlling the pay status of an employee on an approved leave of absence.

- The human resources department must be notified of the date the employee returns to work in order to reinstate the regular pay status.

Salary Continuance for Salaried Employees

Salary continuance provides temporary income for a disabled employee. To be eligible for this coverage, the employee must have worked for the Company for 3 continuous months and must be a regular, full-time, salaried employee.

To qualify for benefits, the employee must be wholly and continuously disabled because of an injury or sickness, unable to perform the duties of his or her occupation, not engaged in any activity for wage or profit, have exhausted his or her sick pay allowance, and be under the care of a doctor.

If the employee has qualified, he or she will begin receiving his or her full base salary on the first day of disability, according to the accompanying schedule.

The employee must provide the human resources department with a written verification of illness signed by a licensed doctor.

Benefits will be reduced by any amount the employee is eligible to receive from other sources of disability income, such as workers' compensation, Social Security, or similarly legislated benefits.

Amount of Benefits

Length of Employment	Weeks at Full Pay	Weeks at Half Pay
3 mos.-1 year	1	3
1 year-2 years	2	6
2 years-3 years	3	9
3 years-4 years	4	12
4 years-5 years	5	16
5 years and over	6	20

The employee must provide the human resources department with a written verification of illness signed by a licensed doctor.

Benefits will be reduced by any amount the employee is eligible to receive from other sources of disability income, such as workers' compensation, Social Security, or similarly legislated benefits.

Employee Performance Appraisal

Today's Date_____

Employee Name _____

Job Title _____

Department/Division _____

Date Position Assumed _____

Employment Date _____

Appraiser's Name _____

Job Title
(of appraiser)_____

Department/Division
(of appraiser)_____

Date Position Assumed
(of appraiser)_____

Performance appraisal must evaluate the performance of the employee on the job for the review period. Performance appraisal comments are restricted to include work that affects job performance, the position's work activities and job duties, and the specified work results that are required for acceptable performance.

Performance appraisal must define those aspects of evaluation that differentiate among levels of job performance. In other words, a rater needs to justify the job related to his or her rating.

When evaluating this employee, remember you are appraising performance for the entire period of the review. It is recommended that you develop a system of monitoring results during the evaluation period so the appraisal reflects the full period's performance.

What work performance strengths does this person have? Please list.

What areas of development do you feel would strengthen this person's job performance, and what are your specific plans to accomplish this development?

Rater's Signature_____

Title_____

Date_____

Rater's Supervisor's_____

Title_____

Date_____

Signature_____

Personnel Review_____

Title_____

Date_____

Employee Comments:

I have read this completed appraisal and discussed my job performance with the rater on_____ (date). I wish to make the following comments:

Employee Signature_____
My signature does not necessarily mean I agree with this performance appraisal.

Salary Adjustment Request

Part One—General Information

Requested increase for:_____
Time in current:
Position
Time with company:_____
Last increase amount:_____% Date:_____ By:_____
This increase is requested by:_____
Title:_____
Date:_____

Part Two—Overall Evaluation

Outstanding Performance
Very Good Performance
Good Performance
Performance must improve to meet requirement of job

Part Three—Salary Information

Job trade:_____
Grade minimum:_____
Grade midpoint:_____
Grade maximum:_____
Grade range:_____

Part Four—Salary Adjustment Proposal

Current salary:_____ Current place in range:_____
Proposed merit increase:_____
Proposed place in range:_____
(Current/proposed salary minus grade minimum divided by grade range)

Proposed salary:_____

* Use next sheet to make comments on the evaluation and increase proposal.

Comments:

_____
Immediate Supervisor Date

Comments:

_____

Next Level Supervisor Date

Human Resources Department:_____

Date received:_____

Action Taken:

Business Analysis Work Sheet

Determine how successful you will be if you enter a given business and sell a given product. Assign each business opportunity and product a column number. Answer questions along the left hand side of the form assigning a rating of 1 - 5, with 5 being the strongest. Total each column when you've finished. The opportunity and product with the highest total points are your strongest candidates for success.

Business Opportunity	Business 1	Business 2	Business 3	Business 4
Relevance of your previous experience to opportunity				
Familiarity with the daily operations of this type of business				
Compatibility of business with your investment goals				
Compatibility of business with your income goals				
Likely profitability of business				
Likelihood of business to meet your desire for personal fulfillment				
Projected growth for the industry				
Acceptability of risk level				
Acceptability of hours you will need to work				
Column Totals				

Product Marketability	Product 1	Product 2	Product 3	Product 4
Probability of one key target market				
Compatibility with image desired				
Competitiveness of price				
Number and strength of marketable features				
Probability that product will enhance sales of current line				
Projected stability of demand				
Ability to overcome seasonal or cyclical resistance				
Uniqueness of product				
Ability of business to obtain needed equipment				
Likely acceptance potential				
Ability of business to afford the development and production of product				
Column totals				
Scores	Total			

Business Name Brainstorm

List three ideas based on the products or services you plan to provide (e.g., children's clothing, custom menu design, business consulting products):

1._____

2._____

3._____

List three ideas based on your special niche (e.g., affordable children's special occasion clothes, exclusive designs for the small restaurateur, business consulting for the office environment):

1._____

2._____

3._____

List three ideas based on your special niche (e.g., affordable children's special occasion clothes, exclusive designs for the small restaurateur, business consulting for the office environment):

1._____

2._____

3._____

List three ideas combining a favorite theme with your special niche: (e.g., Liberty Party children's party clothes, Table For Two menu designs, The Effective Desk business consulting office products):

1._____

2._____

3._____

After you've decided which name you like best, ask yourself a few important questions:

- Have you said it aloud to make sure it's easily understood and pronounced? (Has it passed muster with your family? Have you had a friend call to see how it sounds over the phone?)

- Have you checked your local Yellow Pages to make sure the same or a similar name is not already listed?
- Have you checked with your local business authority to make sure the name is available?
- Have you started your trademark search?

Delegation Checklist

Respond to the following statements. If you are not sure how to answer, put a question mark. Write any additional responses just next to the statements in the "comments" column.

Yes **No**   **Comments**

I delegate appropriate amounts of work to my employees.

I sometimes ask my employees to outline their ideas on a subject before they report to me.

I outline what is expected when I delegate activities to others, and I clearly state the standard of performance I expect.

I recognize that my employees sometimes may see my delegating as a waste of their time, and I seek to clear this up with them.

I have established a framework that my employees understand and agree to.

I sometimes ask employees what I am doing that wastes their time.

I encourage my employees to take initiative as long as they keep me properly informed.

From time to time, I review my delegating style to avoid falling into the trap of over-delegating or under-delegating.

If you answered "yes" to these delegation questions, you are probably delegating effectively. If you answered "no" to some of them, you have areas that need improvement.

Demographic Comparison Work Sheet

To see if the community you are considering offers a population with the demographic traits you need to support your business, fill out the following form.

Population	Market A	Market B	Market C
Within 1 mile of your business			
Within 5 miles of your business			
Within 25 miles of your business			

Income	Market A	Market B	Market C
Under $15,000			
$15,000 - $25,000			
$25,000 - $35,000			
$35,000 - $50,000			
$50,000 - $100,000			
$100,000+			

Age	Market A	Market B	Market C
Preteen			
Teens			
20 - 29			
30 - 39			
40 - 49			
50 - 59			
60 - 69			
70 +			

Density	Market A	Market B	Market C
Unincorporated			
Suburban			
Urban			

General Market Survey

1. Are you:

    Male   Female

2. What is your age?

    18-24   25-34

    35-44   45-54

    55-64   65 or over

3. What is the highest level of formal education you have completed? (Please check only one.)

    Attended High School   Graduated High School

    Attended College   Graduated College

    Post-Graduate Study Without Degree   Post-Graduate Degree

4. What is your marital status

    Married   Single, Never Married

    Separated or Divorced   Widowed

5. How many children under the age of 18 live in your household?

    _____

6. What is your total annual personal income? (Include income from all sources—salary, bonuses, investment income, rents, royalties, etc. Please check only one.)

    Less than $30,000 $30,000-$39,999

    $40,000-$49,999 $50,000-$59,999

    $60,000-$74,999 $75,000-$99,999

    $100,00-$149,999 $150,000-249,999

    $250,000-$499,999 $500,000-$999,999

    $1 million or more

7. In which state and ZIP code area is your main residence?

    State:_____ ZIP code:_____

8. What is your total annual household income? (Including income for all family members and include all sources—salary, bonuses, investment income, rents, royalties, etc. Please check only one.)

Less than $30,000 $30,000-$39,999

$40,000-$49,999 $50,000-$59,999

$60,000-$74,999 $75,000-$99,999

$100,00-$149,999 $150,000-249,999

$250,000-$499,999 $500,000-$999,999

$1 million or more

9a. Do you own a home, condominium or co-op as your primary residence?

Yes   No

9b. If "Yes," what is the present market5 value of your primary residence?

Under $100,000 $100,000-$199,999

$200,000-299,999 $300,000-$499,999

$500,000-$749,999 $750,000-$999,999

$1 million-$1.9 million $2 million or more

If $2 million or more, please estimate value:_____ (Please specify)

10. Do you own a second home, condominium or co-op?

Yes   No

11. What is the total net worth of yourself and all members of your household? Include the estimated market value of your business if you own one, all real estate, including primary residence, car, houschold possessions, bank accounts, stocks, bonds and other investments and assets.

Less than $50,000 $50,000-$99,999

$100,000-$249,999 $250,000-$449,999

$500,000-$749,999 $750,000-$999,999

$1 million-$1.4 million $1.5 million-$1.9 million

$2 million-$4.9 million $5million-$9.9 million

$10 million and over

Home Office Work Sheet

Use this handy work sheet to locate and design your home office

List three possible locations in your home for your office, which should include a work area for you and enough space for your desk, computer and telephone.

1._____
2._____
3._____

Make a physical survey of each location:

- Are phone and electrical outlets placed so that your equipment can easily access them? Or will you be faced with unsightly, unsafe cords snaking across the carpet?
- Measure your space. Will your current desk or table (or the one you have your eye on) fit?
- Do you have adequate lighting? If not, can you create or import it? Is there proper ventilation?
- What is the noise factor?
- Is there room to spread out your work?
- Optional: How close is it to the coffeemaker? Refrigerator? (This can be either a plus or minus, depending on your current jitter factor and waistline.)

Next, list three possible home locations for your inventory:

1._____
2._____
3._____

- Again, make a survey of each location:
- Is it climate-controlled? Will you need climate control?
- Is there adequate lighting, ventilation and space for you to easily access your inventory?
- Will you need to construct special shelving or add other storage space?
  If so, make notes here:

_____
_____
_____

Market Planning Checklist

Before you launch a market campaign, answer the following questions about your business and your product or service.

Have you analyzed the market for your product or service? Do you know which features of your product or service will appeal to different market segments?

In forming your marketing message, have you described how your product or service will benefit your clients?

Have you prepared a pricing schedule? What kinds of discounts do you offer, and to whom do you offer them?

Have you prepared a sales forecast?

What type of media will you use in your marketing campaign?

Have you planned any sales promotions?

Have you planned a publicity campaign?

Do your marketing materials mention any optional accessories or added services that consumers might want to purchase?

If you offer a product, have you prepared clear operating and assembly instructions? What kind of warranty do you provide? What type of customer service or support do you offer after the sale?

Do you have product liability insurance?

Is your style of packaging likely to appeal to your target market?

If your product is one you can patent, have you do so?

How will you distribute your produce?

Have you prepared job descriptions for all of the employees needed to carry out your marketing plans?

Mission Statement

To develop an effective mission statement, ask yourself these questions:

- Why does my company exist? Who do we serve? What is our purpose?

_____

_____

_____

- What are our strengths, weaknesses, opportunities and threats?

_____

_____

_____

- Considering the above, along with your expertise and resources, what business should we be in?

_____

_____

_____

- What is important to us? What do we stand for?

_____

_____

_____

- Now that you've answered those questions, you are ready to write your own mission statement. Use the area below:

_____

_____

_____

_____

_____

Motivation Survey

1. How knowledgeable are you about computer?

    Very   Somewhat

    Slightly   Not at all

2. Which of the following are important to you when evaluating a computer equipment purchase? Check all that apply.

    After-sale support   Attractive product

    Best price for features   Brand name

    Easy to use   hardware compatibility

    Lowest price available   Most features/functions

    Newest technology available   Product quality

    Reputation of vendor   Compact size

    Warranty Other:_____ (please specify)

3. Which of the following sources of information do you use to make decisions about computer or software purchases? (Please check all that apply.)

    Business Publications   Catalogs

    Colleagues   Consultants

    In-store displays   Manufacturer's reps

    PC Publications   Personal experience/knowledge

    Radio   Television

    Trade shows   Newspaper

    Other:_____ (please specify)

4. Which of the following publications do you rely on for information regarding your business or your plans to start a business? (Please check all that apply.)

    Business Nation   Home Office Computing

    Business Week   Inc.

    Byte   Independent Business

Computer Shopper	MacCentral
Computerworld	Macworld Online
Entrepreneur	PC Magazine
eWeek	PC Novice
Forbes	PC World
Fortune	None of these

5. As a small-business owner, please check those of the following topics covered in Entrepreneur magazine that you consider useful.

Tax information	New ideas for business
Financial (raising money, etc.)	Computer technology
Marketing strategies	Company profiles
Latest office equipment	Management tips
Franchise information	Latest small-business trends and statistics
All of the above	None of these

6. Are you:

   Male   Female

7. What is your total annual household income? (Include income from all family members and all sources—salary, bonuses, investment income, tents, royalties, etc.

Less than $30,000	$30,000-$39,999
$40,000-49,999	$50,000-$59,999
$60,000-$74,999	$75,000-$99,999
$100,000-149,999	$150,999-249,999
$250,999-499,999	$500,000-$999,999
$1 million or more	

Performance Evaluation

Employee: _____   Date Hired: _____

Job Title: _____   Salary: _____   Date Of Review: _____

Interaction With Co-workers:

Professional Attributes:

Quality Of Work:

Mutual Improvement Objectives:

Additional Comments:

Date Of Next Evaluation _____

_____   _____
Employee   Supervisor

Performance Report

Employee   Date Hired
Job Title   Salary   Date Of Review

Evaluation Of Performance   **S/W**   **Comments**
Team Player

Meets Deadlines

Organizational Skills

Communication Skills

Leadership Ability

Interaction With Co-workers

Attendance

Quality Of Work

%Strength, Weaknesses

Employer's Comments

Goals

Date Of Next Evaluation ....

_____   _____
Employee   Supervisor

Personal Goals Work Sheets

This work sheet will help you identify the reasons why you want to go into business. Answer each question by rating its level of importance to you, on a scale of 1 to 10, with 1 being least important. Check this list regularly against your business plans. Are you true to yourself?

Lifestyle
I want to provide myself with a reliable job for life.
I want to be my own boss.
I want to be with my family more (probably not possible with anything but a true business).
I want to set my own schedule.
I want to have more time with my kids.
I want to create fame and recognition.

Income
I want to make a reliable living.
- Annual compensation over $75,000
- Annual compensation over $100,000
- Annual compensation over $200,000
- Annual compensation over $500,000

I want to eventually sell my business for a high price.
- For over $100,000
- For over $250,000
- For over $500,000
- For over $1,000,000

I want to take large risks for large financial rewards.
- Annual sales over $100,000
- Annual sales over $250,000
- Annual sales over $500,000
- Annual sales over $1,000,000

Style Of Business
I want to build a big business and then sell it.
I want to start a business that doesn't require employees.
I want to make decisions regarding my business without anyone looking over my shoulder.
I want to build a business I can pass on to my family.
I want to manage a good team of employees.

Other Issues
I want to offer better jobs to others than I've had myself.
I want my company to be as socially as well as environmentally responsible.

Record Of Disciplinary Action

Employee Name: Employee Title:
Manager Name: Manager Title:
Today's Date: Incident Date:
Incident Time: Incident Location:

Description of the incident that occurred:

_____
_____
_____
_____
_____
_____
_____
_____

Witnesses to the incident (if applicable)

_____
_____
_____
_____
_____

Names of those in attendance at current disciplinary action meeting:

_____
_____
_____
_____
_____

Corrective or disciplinary action to be taken:

Verbal Written Probation Suspension Other (explain below)

_____
_____
_____
_____
_____
_____
_____

(If probation, period begins _____ and ends
_____.)

Goals to be achieved:

_____

_____

_____

_____

_____

Consequences for failure to improve performance or correct behavior:

_____

_____

_____

_____

_____

Prior discussions or warnings on this subject, whether oral or written:

_____

_____

_____

_____

_____

Employee statement:

_____

_____

_____

_____

_____

_____

_____

_____

_____

I acknowledge that I have read and understand the above information and consequences.

_____

Employee Signature Date

_____

Supervisor Signature Date

Sales Representative Evaluation Checklist

Many small companies are unable to field a large sales force, so they enhance their efforts by using independent sales representatives who will sell their products, along with those of other businesses, for a contracted commission. This checklist will help you evaluate each representative you will be considering.

Does the rep carry conflicting or competing lines?
What is the rep's commission structure?
Where is the showroom, if any? How about the warehouse?
What is the geographical area covered?
Who is the rep's key account?
What is the number of salespeople?
How many years has the rep been in business?
What type of promotional support is offered?
How willing is the rep to submit sales-call reports?
How frequent are the rep's trade-show appearances?
What is the rep's specialty?
Has the rep listed all markets covered?
Can the rep personally interview field sales reps?
Does the rep really know the customer?
Can the rep provide a termination agreement?
When are commissions paid?
When are overdue accounts collected?
What deductions does the rep make for credit losses?
What rights does the rep have as far as credit rejection is concerned?
What catalogs or other materials are required?
Can you appear at sales meetings, to see how things go?
Will reps buy samples at deep discounts?
Does the rep warehouse any inventory?
Can the rep supply a current list of references?

Self-Assessment Work Sheet

Complete the following self-assessment work sheet as honestly as you can. Just write down whatever comes to mind; don't over-think the exercise. Most likely, your first response will be your best. Once you've finished the exercise, look for partners (i.e., is there a need for a business dong one of the things you like or are good at?

1. List at least five to seven things you like to do or are good at.

_____

_____

_____

_____

_____

_____

_____

2. List five to seven things you are not good at or you don't like to do.

_____

_____

_____

_____

_____

_____

_____

3. If there were three to five products or services that would make my personal life better, what would they be?

_____

_____

_____

_____

_____

_____

_____

4. If there were three to five products or services that would make my business life better, what would they be?

_____

_____

_____

_____

_____

_____

_____

5. When people ask what you do, what's your answer (list one occupation or whatever mainly occupies your week)?

_____

_____

_____

_____

_____

_____

_____

6. List five things you enjoy about your work.

_____

_____

_____

_____

_____

_____

_____

7. List five things you dislike about your work.

_____

_____

_____

_____

_____

_____

_____

8. When people tell me what they like most about me, their response is:

_____

_____

_____

_____

_____

_____

_____

9. Some people dislike the fact that I:

_____

_____

_____

_____

_____

_____

10. Other than your main occupation, list any other skills you possess, whether you excel at them or not:

_____

_____

_____

_____

_____

_____

_____

11. In addition to becoming more financially independent, I would also like to be more:

_____

_____

_____

_____

_____

_____

12. Write down three things you want to see changed or improved in your community.

_____

_____

_____

_____

_____

_____

_____

Self-Evaluation

Answer the following questions by checking the appropriate box to the right. After you have finished answering each question, total the number of checked boxes in each column. Multiply the total of each column by the severity factor for that category. Add together the total of each column. This is your evaluation score. The higher the score, the better your understanding is of your company, its structure and your role in it.

		Below Average (1)	Satisfactory (2)	Above Average (3)	Superior (4)
1	I know what the responsibilities of my job are.				
2	I know who my supervisor is and what he or she is.				
3	I feel my workload is too heavy.				
4	I feel I can discuss my problems with my superior.				
5	I know what my benefits are.				
6	I feel that I am a part of a productive work team.				
7	I always know what my daily and weekly goals are.				
8	I know what the long-term goals of the company are.				
9	I feel I have had enough training to perform my job.				
	Total the number of responses in each column.				
	Multiply the responses by each column's severity factor.				
	Add the results for your total audit score.				

Strategic Planning Checklist

A strategic planning meeting should be held at least once a year and should include executive managers as well as any key supervisor with front- line knowledge and experience. Bring a copy of your company's business plan to the meeting so it can be referred to when needed. Keep in mind the purpose of the meeting, which is to evaluate past projects and goals and to develop new strategies based on opportunities discovered through market research and analysis.

The following list can help create a more effective strategic planning meeting:

The meeting should be held off-site in a casual setting so participants will feel relaxed but away from distractions.

Make sure everyone knows that each person will be treated as an equal and everyone will have an equal voice in terms of suggestions and criticisms.

To promote a more comfortable atmosphere, have everyone dress in casual clothing.

Encourage discussion of subjects mentioned in the meeting. This will not only encourage more brainstorming as the meeting progresses, but it will also serve to fully define the subject and determine its merits.

Don't let the meeting digress into endless criticism. Point out areas that merit praises, and when discussing areas of weakness, explain how certain suggestions may not fit into the overall scope of the company's strategy.

Don't try to prioritize items brought up in the meeting. The strategic planning meeting is mainly a brainstorming session where ideas are explored in relation to their strategic impact on the business.

Don't assume that everyone will come with a notepad and pen. Make sure you provide both.

Make sure you cover each topic thoroughly before progressing to the next. Keep in mind that you are exploring strategic solutions.

When discussing each subject, apply timelines for specific actions after the meeting has been adjourned.

Write a summary of the meeting and circulate it to everyone who is part of the strategic planning team. Then, make sure you have follow-up meetings to review each person's progress.

Target Market Work Sheet

1. Describe the idea:

2. What will the concept be used for?

3. Where are similar concepts used and sold?

4. What places do my prospects go to for recreation?

5. Where do my prospects go for education?

6. Where do my prospects do their shopping?

7. What types of newspapers, magazines, and newsletters do my prospects read?

8. What TV and radio stations do my prospects watch and listen to?

Code of Conduct

The company prides itself on the high standards of excellence embodied by our operating principles. We expect our employees to personify these ideals in their dealing with persons both inside and outside the company. The following code of conduct is intended to provide guidelines for the professional, ethical, legal, and socially responsible behavior we expect of our employees.

It is impossible for this code to cover every situation that may arise. When you have a question, ask your supervisor or the ethics officer. In circumstances where you are unable to consult with an appropriate person in the company, use your common sense and good judgment.

I. Professional Integrity

Consistent with our operating principles, employees should strive to conduct all business dealings and relationships with integrity, honesty, and respect for others. Employees should loyally and faithfully serve our principles and always deal fairly and honestly with customers and others with whom we do business. No employee should knowingly permit any transaction to occur through his or her offices that is not fair to our principals and customers alike.

Relationships with customers, manufacturers, suppliers, competitors, and employees are to be based on fair dealing, on fair competition in quality, price, and service, and on compliance with applicable laws and regulations.

II. Accurate and Complete Accounting

A. Employees should use a manufacturer's funds and other property solely for the benefit of that manufacturer. All disbursements must be lawful and consistent with instructions provided by the manufacturer. Transactions concerning the account, including the purchase and distribution of premiums, should be clearly authorized and properly and promptly recorded.

B. No unrecorded fund, reserve, asset, or special account shall be set up or maintained for any purpose. No false or fictitious entries shall be made in books, records, accounts, or in company communications for any reason. No payment or transfer of funds or assets (such as tangible and intangible premiums) shall be made for any purpose other than that described by the supporting documents, and specifically as authorized by the principal or clearly within the discretion granted to the company by the principal.

C. Employees are responsible for accurate and timely recordkeeping for all company assets, liabilities, revenues, and expenses. Compliance with accepted accounting rules and controls is required. All books, records, and documents must accurately and completely describe the transactions they represent.

III. Bribes and Kickbacks

1. The company does not permit or condone bribes, kickbacks, or any other illegal, secret, or improper payments, transfers, or receipts. This prohibition applies both to the giving and the receiving of payments or gifts.

2. All payments and transfers of premium and other items of value to employees of other business entities or to such entities themselves shall be made openly and must be disclosed and authorized in advance by the principal, the customer, and the company.

3. No employee shall offer, give, or transfer any money or anything else of value for the personal benefit of any employee or agent of another business entity for the purpose of:

4.Obtaining or retaining any business that the business entity itself would not otherwise provide

5. Receiving any kind of favored treatment that the business entity itself would not otherwise provide

6. Inducing or assisting such employee or agent to violate any duty to his employer or to violate any law.

7. No employee shall assist in the misuse of manufacturers' or company funds, including, without limitation, the misappropriation of such funds for the personal benefit of employees of the manufacturer, the company, or customers.

8. No outside agent of any kind shall be used to circumvent the prohibition against bribes, kickbacks, and other illegal, secret, or improper payments. Fees, commissions, and expenses paid to outside agents must be based upon proper billings, accurate recordkeeping, and reasonable standards for services rendered.

HUMAN RESOURCES GLOSSARY

This glossary contains terms you may run across in your job, especially those terms with some legal connection. Not included are very common words or words that usually have their ordinary dictionary meaning.

A

Accommodation: any change or adjustment to a job or work environment that permits a qualified applicant or employee with a disability to participate in the job application process, to perform the essential functions of a job, or to enjoy benefits and privileges of employment equal to those enjoyed by employees without disabilities.

Affirmative action plan: a management tool designed to ensure equal employment opportunity in hiring, compensation, promotion, and termination.

Alternative dispute resolution (ADR): a method used to resolve a dispute out of court. Mediation and arbitration are two common forms of ADR.

Annuity: a payment of money that is made yearly for the life of the person who is entitled to the payment.

Antitrust law: a state or federal statute that restricts monopolistic practices, anticompetitive practices, and other restraints of trade.

Applicant: an individual who has submitted a résumé and/or completed a job application either in person or by mail or via Internet in response to a job posting, advertisement, or other notice of a job opening.

Arbitration: a method of dispute resolution in which the parties agree to present evidence and arguments to a neutral umpire (or team of umpires) and abide by the umpire's decision.

Assistive devices: items specifically designed to meet job-related disability accommodations, rather than personal needs.

Attrition: loss of employees (as a result of resignation, retirement, death) who are not replaced by their employer, thus reducing the size of that employer's workforce.

At-will employment: the traditional relationship between employees and employers, where employees have no legal right to keep their jobs.

Audit: an investigation, especially a review of records and procedures, whose purpose is to assess compliance with a legal or practical requirement.

B

Back pay: earnings granted to an employee, usually by a court that represent the difference between wages already paid the employee and higher wages to which he or she was entitled but did not receive. (Back pay is often awarded in cases of proven discrimination.)

Bargaining unit: a group of employees who, by reason of the similarity of their jobs, form a unit appropriate for bargaining with management on questions of wages, benefits, and working conditions.

Beneficiary: a person, several persons, or trust designated to receive benefits from a plan at the participant's death.

Bona fide occupational qualification (BFOQ): a specific job-related requirement that is legitimate and considered a precursor to hiring a candidate for a position. Race cannot be a BFOQ, but gender, age, religion, or national origin may be claimed as a BFOQ provided that reasonable proof exists for such a claim.

Breach of contract: failure to perform as required under a valid agreement with another party.

Business necessity: specific job-related requirement that is considered by the employer to be essential to the mission of the business; sometimes used as a defense against discrimination claims regarding employee selection.

C

Cafeteria benefits/plan: a benefit plan in which an employee can pick and choose among a number of fringe benefits up to a designated dollar amount in addition to the universal benefits granted to all employees.

Casual workers: those not working in the usual course of the employer's business (e.g., a carpet installer, carpenter), but on an "as needed" basis.

Collective bargaining: a procedure for attaining agreement with an employer on matters involving wages, benefits, and working conditions by a group of employees or their representative.

Comparable worth: the belief that employees in comparable positions should receive equal pay.

Comparable worth theory: a theory of pay structures requiring that jobs that, though not similar in duties, are of comparable economic value to the employer, should carry equal rates of pay. Some states require that comparable worth jobs be paid equally, particularly in the public sector.

Compensatory damages: money that is awarded in a judicial proceeding to compensate a party for injury to person or property.

Conciliation: the settlement of a conflict in an amicable fashion.

Consent order: a court order entered with the consent of all parties to a judicial proceeding. A settlement that has been adopted by a court.

Contingent workers: workers, such as agency temporaries, contract employees, leased employees, and direct hires, whose jobs are structured to last only a certain length of time.

Covered entity: an employer, employment agency, labor organization, or joint labor-management committee.

D

Damages: money or other compensation recovered in the courts by any person who has suffered a loss.

Debarment: an exclusion or preclusion from something; in business terms, usually refers to an exclusion from subcontracting with the government.

Defamation: any intentionally false statement that has been communicated to another and that tends to hold a person up to contempt, ridicule, or ill-repute. A defamatory statement can form the grounds for a lawsuit. A defamatory statement is a libel if it is written and a slander if it is communicated orally.

Defined benefit plans: A retirement plan in which the employer makes contributions to employees' individual accounts and the final benefit consists solely of investments and returns that have accumulated in the individual accounts.

Disability: a physical or mental impairment that substantially limits one or more of a person's major life activities.

Disclaimer: a statement repudiating or renouncing a claim or representation.

Disclosure: a revelation of something; the uncovering of a fact previously hidden or unknown.

Discrimination: adverse, unlawful employment action taken against an applicant or employee because of his or her race, sex, color, religion, national origin, disability, age, or veteran status.

Disparate impact: a disproportionate adverse effect on a particular disadvantaged group.

Disqualifying events: failure or refusal to provide necessary information.

Domestic partners: unmarried heterosexual or homosexual couples who are living together and dependent on each other financially, emotionally, and in other ways, but are not "married" as defined by state law.

Downsizing: a euphemism used for cutting back on the number of employees; a layoff of workers.

Due process of law: any set of legal procedures that is guaranteed to a party to a legal proceeding by virtue of a statute, constitution, or judicial decision.

E

Employee assistance programs (EAPs): employer-sponsored programs designed to provide counseling for problems concerning health, marital difficulties, alcohol and drug abuse, stress, or other things that may affect an employee's work performance.

Early retirement: retirement that commences before the designated standard age of retirement, which is usually accompanied by lesser pension benefits. In some cases, however, companies will offer early retirement programs as a way to avoid layoffs and, for purposes of incentive, benefits are not diminished.

EEO-1 form: form required by the U.S. Department of Labor for employers with 100 or more employees. Summarizes workforce by job category, race, and color.

Employment-at-will: an employment arrangement that grants employers the right to fire employees for any reason or for no reason at all, and likewise, allows employees to quit their jobs at any time for any reason.

Equal pay theory: the theory that men and women should be paid equally for performing equal work, made into law by the federal Equal Pay Act.

Ergonomics: pertaining to an arrangement of physical tasks and the work environment in such a way as to accommodate the functions and limitations of the human body.

Essential functions: duties that are basic or fundamental to a position; under ADA, reasonable accommodation must be made in order for a qualified individual with a disability to perform the essential functions of a position.

Exempt employee: employees who perform certain types of work and who are paid a predetermined amount each pay period. With limited exception, exempt employees must receive full salary for any week in which they perform any work.

Exit interview: an interview with an employee who is leaving the company; such a meeting gives the employee an opportunity to pass along information regarding healthcare coverage and other benefits. The employer is also able to ask employees about their reason for leaving and their opinion of the company, which may be helpful to the employer regarding future employee policies and relations.

Experience rating: a figure used by workers' compensation insurers and state unemployment authorities in calculating premium rates or contribution rates that makes appropriate adjustments to reflect an employer's claims history.

F

Fair employment practice: a manner of operating in which there is no discrimination on the basis of factors that do not apply to job performance, such as race, gender, and religion, in employment practices.

Family and Medical Leave: usually granted pursuant to state or federal law; gives employees job-protected unpaid time off after the birth or adoption of a child, for personal illness, to care for a sick family member, because of any qualifying exigency arising out of covered military duty of a family member (or notification of an impending call or order to active military duty), or to care for a family member who is seriously ill or injured as a result of his or her covered military service. The terms and conditions of such leaves vary depending on federal and state law and/or employer policies.

Fiduciary: a trustee; a person to whom money or property had been turned over to be managed and taken proper care of for the benefit of others.

Flexible spending account (FSA): an account set up for employees by an employer as a benefit plan, to which employees contribute a portion of their gross earnings each month. Employees can make withdrawals from these accounts to pay for specified expenses (but lose any funds they do not spend at the end of the year).

G

Garnishment: an order from a judicial or governmental agency requiring an employer to withhold a certain sum from the wages of an employee for payment of a debt.

Good faith: honesty and without deception; the duty to act fairly and equitably.

Government contractor: a company that presently holds a contract for goods or services with the state or an Executive agency of the federal government, or intends to apply to supply goods or services for government business.

Green card: another term for a USCIS Alien Registration Receipt Card (Form I-151 or I-551), an immigrant visa that allows a foreign-born noncitizen to become a permanent resident of the United States and lawfully secure work.

Grievance: an oral or legal statement that outlines an alleged violation, misinterpretation, or inequitable application of a particular term or provision of personnel policies or, in a unionized workplace, an existing collective bargaining agreement.

Gross misconduct: behavior that causes someone to lose his or her job as the result of actions that are more serious than poor performance or judgment.

H

Honesty test: any of a number of psychological surveys that attempt to expose an individual's tendency to be dishonest.

Hostile environment: a term used for the result of sexual harassment that creates an abusive or intimidating working environment for the person being harassed.

I

Impairment: a physiological disorder affecting one or more body systems or a mental or psychological disorder.

Implied contract: a legal relation in which mutual obligations may be inferred, without formal agreement, simply from the conduct of the parties and their mutual understandings and expectations.

Independent contractor: a worker who individually contracts with an employer to provide specialized or requested services on a project or as- needed basis, but is not an employee.

Indexing: the periodic and automatic adjustment of employee compensation to account for inflation in the economy.

J

Jurisdiction: the power of a court to decide disputes; the geographical area over which a court's power extends.

L

Leave allotment: refers to the total number of weeks of leave eligibility granted to an eligible employee per year under applicable leave laws; e.g., the leave allotment for eligible employees under federal Family and Medical Leave law is 12 weeks per 12-month period.

Leave bank: (sometimes referred to as a paid time off or PTO bank) 1. a lump disbursement of a certain number of days or hours of leave, from which an employee can draw time and self-designate it as vacation time, sick time, personal leave, etc; 2. a bank maintained by the employer to which employees can "donate" vacation or sick time, to be used by co- workers with catastrophic illnesses requiring extensive time off the job. Some employers maintain leave banks on an ongoing basis, others establish such banks on a case-by-case basis when a particular employee is in need of extended leave.

Liability: a debt; a disadvantage; vulnerability to a lawsuit.

Libel: a defamatory statement that is published (i.e., disclosed to another person) in writing.

Lump-sum distribution: payment of an entire amount due all at one time (as opposed payment in installments or annuity payments).

M

Major life activity: a function including caring for oneself, performing manual tasks, seeing, hearing, eating, sleeping, walking, standing, lifting, bending, speaking, breathing, learning, reading, concentrating, thinking, communicating, and working. In addition, major life activity also includes the operation of a major bodily system, including the digestive, neurological, respiratory, circulatory, endocrine, reproductive, and immune systems; the functioning of the bowels, bladder, and brain; and normal cell growth.

Mediation: a method of dispute resolution in which the parties present evidence and arguments to an impartial third party whose obligation is to help bring about an agreed settlement.

Metrics: a means to quantify, measure, and track key performance indicators.

N

National origin: a term that refers to the country in which a person was born or from which his or her ancestors came; discrimination based on national origin is considered a violation of an individual's civil rights.

Negligence: the failure to use proper care.

Negligent referral: a failure by the former (or soon-to-be-former) employer of an employee to inform future potential employers of job-related negative information regarding that employee, when acting as a reference on their behalf.

Nepotism: the employment of relatives and friends of the employer and of other employees.

No-fault leave policy: a leave policy in which employees are automatically terminated after they have been on leave for a certain amount of time, regardless of the reason for taking the leave.

Non-compete agreement: an agreement between an employer and an employee that states that if the employee leaves the company, he or she will be barred from working for a company that competes with the current employer's business, work within a certain distance of the employer, or both, for a specified time.

O

Outplacement: providing help to terminated employees in finding new employment.

P

Paid time off (PTO) bank: (see Leave Bank)

Pay compression: when an employee is at the top of the pay range for his or her job grade.

Pecuniary: monetary, financial, usually used to identify the type of damages awarded to a plaintiff.

Peer review: a procedure for handling employee grievances in which a committee consisting of representatives of employees and management hear and decide all grievances.

Per diem: per day; an amount of money that is payable per day.

Piecework: a method of employee compensation in which the employee is paid for output (by the "piece") rather than for time (by the hour).

"Portal-to-portal": short for the Portal-to-Portal Act, which relieved employers of the obligation to pay employees for time spent traveling to and from the worksite.

Preemption: the supremacy of federal law over state law; the unenforceability of a particular state law due to the existence of a supervening federal law.

Preexisting condition: a condition (usually physical) of an employee that exists prior to the commencement of health care under a group medical plan.

Premium: an amount of money paid for the purchase of an insurance policy, usually calculated in proportion to the risk insured against.

Prevailing wage: the rate of pay and fringe benefits, as determined by the government, that prevails among workers in a particular occupation and geographical area and that must be paid to workers in similar occupations on projects that are performed under government contracts.

Prima facie: sufficient, in terms of evidence, to establish a fact.

Progressive discipline: a specific set of procedures regarding employee discipline in which disciplinary actions "progress" in their severity at each instance where it becomes necessary to impose it. For example, the first step could be one or more verbal warnings, followed by one or more written warnings, followed by suspension, and finally termination. Practicing consistently applied progressive discipline thwarts both hasty terminations and/or playing favorites on the part of management as well as claims of discrimination on the part of employees.

Prohibited factor: that which cannot be used as criterion for making an employment decision, such as the race, gender, or religion of the candidate.

Proprietary information: that which belongs exclusively to a person or company.

Protected class: a group that is covered by antidiscrimination laws or fair employment practice laws. Covered classes under federal law include race, religion, sex, age, national origin, disabled individuals, and veterans. Some jurisdictions include sexual orientation as a protected class.

Q

Qualified beneficiary: a term used by COBRA that refers to an employee or his/her spouse and/or dependent children when they are eligible to receive coverage under COBRA because healthcare coverage was lost as the result of a qualifying event.

Qualified domestic relations order (QDRO): allows retirement benefits to be paid to a third party.

Qualifying event: a term used by COBRA that refers to specific events that result in an employee or his/her spouse and/or dependents children's loss of health coverage, such as divorce, layoff, or termination. Such events "qualify" that individual or individuals to be covered under COBRA.

R

Recall: the act of bringing employees back to work after a temporary layoff. Usually, recall will proceed on the basis of seniority—those with the most seniority will return to work first—or on a "last to be fired, first to be hired" basis.

Release: a document that relieves a party of legal responsibility toward the signer.

Remuneration: payment for goods provided or services rendered; compensation.

Repetitive motion injury: any bodily injury sustained as a result of repetitive motions over a long period, particularly those performed in connection with employment.

Respond at superior: a legal doctrine that holds the employer responsible for acts committed by employees in the course of their employment.

Restraining order: a court order to refrain from particular conduct; an injunction.

Retaliation: an action taken by an employer that has a negative impact on an employee because the employee has complained about or claimed wrongdoing against the employer.

Return on investment (ROI): a department or process contributing (among overhead functions) to corporate success or profitability.

Reverse discrimination: prejudice exercised against a person or class for the purpose of correcting a pattern of discrimination against another person or class.

S

"Same actor" inference: the claim that if the person who fires an employee was the same person who hired that employee, then it logically follows that there is no basis for a complaint of discrimination against the employer.

Serious health condition: for the purposes of FMLA, an illness, injury, impairment or physical or mental condition that involves either inpatient care (i.e., an overnight stay in a hospital, hospice or residential care facility) or continuing treatment by a healthcare provider.

Service letter: a letter provided to an employee by a former employer, describing the nature and duration of the employment and the reason for termination.

Set-asides: a proportion of government contracts that are reserved for businesses owned by members of disadvantaged groups.

Severance pay: money offered by employers to workers who have been terminated or laid off.

Sexual harassment: an unwelcome behavior of a sexual nature that explicitly or implicitly affects a term or condition of an individual's employment, unreasonably interferes with an employee's work performance, or creates an intimidating, hostile, or offensive work environment.

Slander: a defamatory statement that is published (i.e., disclosed to another person) orally.

Small necessities: term coined by several states to refer to certain family obligations of workers, such as attending to children's school conferences and pediatrician visits, and/or assisting elderly relatives with doctors' visits and personal care. Several states now mandate that employers give time off to attend to those matters pursuant to small necessities leave laws.

Solicitation: 1) oral communications and the exchange of union authorization cards used to file election petitions with the National Labor Relations Board, or 2) requesting political or charitable donations from employees.

Statute of frauds: the legal requirement that certain contracts (e.g., for the sale of land, for services that cannot be performed within a year) be in writing.

Statutes of limitations: laws that establish deadlines for the institution of various kinds of legal actions.

Strict liability: legal responsibility for injury, without regard to fault.

Strike: a work stoppage by employees in connection with a labor dispute.

Subcontractor: an individual or company that takes on a portion of a contract originally assigned to a primary contractor.

Subsidies: government grants given to businesses, which can occur in a number of ways and for a number of reasons. Generally, the government grants subsidies when they have a vested interest in the company or organization or believe it to be beneficial to the public.

Succession planning: a basic replacement plan that, in effect, is a risk- management device that enables a business to replace a fallen leader.

Summary plan description (SPD): a document that explains the claims procedure and other benefit information of a healthcare insurance plan to employees.

T

Telecommuter: an employee who works at home or an offsite location via computer, often by transfer of electronic data. The employee communicates with the employer by email, telephone, and electronic meeting technologies.

Tenure: incumbency in a job; in academic employment especially, an entitlement to "lifetime" employment that is granted to faculty members who satisfy certain criteria.

Termination for cause: termination of an employee on grounds that any reasonable person would view as justified.

Tort: a negligent or intentional wrong, not arising from a statute or contract, for which a person can be sued.

Transitional workplace: a worksite that occupies workers who are recovering from illness or injury with "light" duties until they regain their ability to resume their regular jobs.

U

Undue hardship: a term that refers to unreasonable or excessive expense or inconvenience that would be necessary on the part of an employer to accommodate an employee.

Union security agreement: a collective bargaining agreement that requires all employees in the bargaining unit to be union members or to pay union dues.

V

Vested benefits: benefits that have been accrued and are, therefore, owned by an employee; not conditional or contingent in any way. Under ERISA, all retirement plans must offer vested benefits.

Vocational rehabilitation: occupational training to facilitate the reassignment of a disabled worker.

W

Waiver: a written or oral acknowledgment that a person has given up a legal right.

Wellness: condition of health based on preventative and preemptive actions of individuals, such as exercise, weight loss, stress prevention, and smoking cessation.

Whistleblower: a person who reports illegal or improper conduct, especially improper conduct on the part of the whistleblower's employer.

Willful: intentional; deliberate.

Workers' compensation: a program that provides fixed payments for wages lost and medical expenses to employees who are injured on the job. Usually, such payments can be extended to a worker's spouse and dependents. This benefits both employees and employers, because incapacitated employees continue to receive income and employers are protected from lawsuits resulting from injured workers.

Workweek: under the Fair Labor Standards Act, a workweek is a period of 168 hours during 7 consecutive 24-hour periods that may begin on any day of the week and at any hour of the day as established by the employer.

Wrongful discharge: a reason for termination of an employee that is not legitimate. A wrongful discharge is usually in violation of law (or the employee handbook).

Notes

1. Theresa M. Welbourne, Ph.D. Impact Factor: 0.93. ISI Journal Citation Reports.

2. Michael Armstrong, Personnel Management Practices, Englewood Cliffs, Prentice-Hall, 1999

3. De Cenzo, A. David, P. Robinson, "Personnel/Human Resource Management", Englewood Cliffs, Prentice-Hall, 1988.

4. Donald W. Myers, "Human Resource Management. Principles and Practice", Commerce Clearing House, Inc., 1986.

5. Jean-Marie Peretti, "Resources Humaines", 10th Edition, editura Vuibert, Paris, 2006

6. R. Wayne Mondy, Robert M. Noe, op. cit., pp 20-26.

7. Prof. Dr. Ion Verboncu, Managementul Organizafiei, Lecture Notes, Academia de Studii Economice, Bucuresti, academic year 2004-2005.

8. Rect. Van-Jesus de Capdam, Organizational Management, Lecture Notes, Open University of Netherland, 2006-2007.

9. Anne-Wil Harzing, Joris van Ruysseveldt, "International Human Resource Management—an Integrated Approach", Open University of the Netherlands, SAGE Publications, 1955 reprinted in 1996, 1998, 1999.

10. Chris Brewster, Wolfgang Mayrhofer, Michael Morley, "Human Resource Management in Europe: Evidence of Convergence", Cranfield University, School of Management, London, May 31st, 2004.

11. Prof. Dr. Aurel Manolescu, "Managementul resurselor umane", Editura RAI, Imprimeria" Coresi", Bucuresti, 1998.

12. IPM, "Statement on Personnel Management and Personnel Policies", in Personnel Management, March 1963.